Top Careers in Two Years

Education and Social Services

Titles in the *Top Careers in Two Years* Series

1 Food, Agriculture, and Natural Resources
2 Construction and Trades
3 Communications and the Arts
4 Business, Finance, and Government Administration
5 Education and Social Services
6 Health Care, Medicine, and Science
7 Hospitality, Human Services, and Tourism
8 Computers and Information Technology
9 Public Safety, Law, and Security
10 Manufacturing and Transportation
11 Retail, Marketing, and Sales

Top Careers in Two Years

Education and Social Services

By Jessica Cohn

Ferguson Publishing
An imprint of Infobase Publishing

Top Careers in Two Years
Education and Social Services

Ferguson
An imprint of Infobase Publishing
132 West 31st Street
New York, NY 10001

ISBN-13: 978-0-8160-6900-2
ISBN-10: 0-8160-6900-X

Library of Congress Cataloging-in-Publication Data

Top careers in two years.
    v. cm.
    Includes index.
    Contents: v. 1. Food, agriculture, and natural resources / by Scott Gillam — v. 2. Construction and trades / Deborah Porterfield — v. 3. Communications and the arts / Claire Wyckoff — v. 4. Business, finance, and government administration / Celia W. Seupal — v. 5. Education and social services / Jessica Cohn — v. 6. Health care, medicine, and science / Deborah Porterfield — v. 7. Hospitality, human services, and tourism / Rowan Riley — v. 8. Computers and information technology / Claire Wyckoff — v. 9. Public safety, law, and security / Lisa Cornelio, Gail Eisenberg — v. 10. Manufacturing and transportation — v. 11. Retail, marketing, and sales / Paul Stinson.
    ISBN-13: 978-0-8160-6896-8 (v. 1 : hc : alk. paper)
    ISBN-10: 0-8160-6896-8 (v. 1 : hc : alk. paper)
    ISBN-13: 978-0-8160-6897-5 (v. 2 : hc. : alk. paper)
    ISBN-10: 0-8160-6897-6 (v. 2 : hc. : alk. paper)
    ISBN-13: 978-0-8160-6898-2 (v. 3 : hc : alk. paper)
    ISBN-10: 0-8160-6898-4 (v. 3 : hc : alk. paper)
    ISBN-13: 978-0-8160-6899-9 (v. 4 : hc : alk. paper)
    ISBN-10: 0-8160-6899-2 (v. 4 : hc : alk. paper)
    ISBN-13: 978-0-8160-6900-2 (v. 5 : hc : alk. paper)
    ISBN-10: 0-8160-6900-X (v. 5 : hc : alk. paper)
    ISBN-13: 978-0-8160-6901-9 (v. 6 : hc : alk. paper)
    ISBN-10: 0-8160-6901-8 (v. 6 : hc : alk. paper)
    ISBN-13: 978-0-8160-6902-6 (v. 7 : hc : alk. paper)
    ISBN-10: 0-8160-6902-6 (v. 7 : hc : alk. paper)
    ISBN-13: 978-0-8160-6903-3 (v. 8 : hc : alk. paper)
    ISBN-10: 0-8160-6903-4 (v. 8 : hc : alk. paper)
    ISBN-13: 978-0-8160-6904-0 (v. 9 : hc : alk. paper)
    ISBN-10: 0-8160-6904-2 (v. 9 : hc : alk. paper)
    ISBN-13: 978-0-8160-6905-7 (v. 10 : hc : alk. paper)
    ISBN-10: 0-8160-6905-0 (v. 10 : hc : alk. paper)
    ISBN-13: 978-0-8160-6906-4 (v. 11 : hc : alk. paper)
    ISBN-10: 0-8160-6906-9 (v. 11 : hc : alk. paper)
    1. Vocational guidance—United States. 2. Occupations—United States. 3. Professions—United States.
    HF5382.5.U5T677 2007
    331.7020973—dc22

                                                                    2006028638

Produced by Print Matters, Inc.
Text design by A Good Thing, Inc.
Cover design by Salvatore Luongo

Printed in the United States of America

Sheridan PMI 10 9 8 7 6 5 4 3 2 1

This book is printed on acid-free paper.

Contents

How to Use This Book   vii

Acknowledgments   ix

Introduction   xi

Chapter **1** Preschool Teacher 1
Chapter **2** Teacher Assistant 10
Chapter **3** Drug and Alcohol Abuse Counselor. 18
Chapter **4** Sign Language Interpreter 27
Chapter **5** Recreation Worker 35
Chapter **6** Child Care Worker. 43
Chapter **7** School Administrative Assistant 52
Chapter **8** Vocational Education Instructor 60
Chapter **9** Library Assistant 68
Chapter **10** Social and Human Services Assistant 76

Appendix A: Tools for Career Success   85

Appendix B: Financial Aid   93

Index   103

How to Use This Book

This book, part of the Top Careers in Two Years series, highlights in-demand careers for readers considering a two-year degree program—either straight out of high school or after working a job that does not require advanced education. The focus throughout is on the fastest-growing jobs with the best potential for advancement in the field. Readers learn about future prospects while discovering jobs they may never have heard of.

An associate's degree can be a powerful tool in launching a career. This book tells you how to use it to your advantage, explore job opportunities, and find local degree programs that meet your needs.

Each chapter provides the essential information needed to find not just a job but a career that fits your particular skills and interests. All chapters include the following features:

- "Vital Statistics" provides crucial information at a glance, such as salary range, employment prospects, education or training needed, and work environment.

- Discussion of salary and wages notes hourly versus salaried situations as well as potential benefits. Salary ranges take into account regional differences across the United States.

- "Keys to Success" is a checklist of personal skills and interests needed to thrive in the career.

- "A Typical Day at Work" describes what to expect at a typical day on the job.

- "Two-Year Training" lays out the value of an associate's degree for that career and what you can expect to learn.

- "What to Look For in a School" provides questions to ask and factors to keep in mind when selecting a two-year program.

- "The Future" discusses prospects for the career going forward.

- "Interview with a Professional" presents firsthand information from someone working in the field.

- "Job Seeking Tips" offers suggestions on how to meet and work with people in the field, including how to get an internship or apprenticeship.

- "Career Connections" lists Web addresses of trade organizations providing more information about the career.

- "Associate's Degree Programs" provides a sampling of some of the better-known two-year schools.

- "Financial Aid" provides career-specific resources for financial aid.

- "Related Careers" lists similar related careers to consider.

In addition to a handy comprehensive index, the back of the book features two appendices providing invaluable information on job hunting and financial aid. Appendix A, Tools for Career Success, provides general tips on interviewing either for a job or two-year program, constructing a strong résumé, and gathering professional references. Appendix B, Financial Aid, introduces the process of applying for aid and includes information about potential sources of aid, who qualifies, how to prepare an application, and much more.

Acknowledgments

Sincere appreciation goes out to all the helpful people who provided background information for this volume and to all those who helped the author make connections with her sources.

Thanks go to, listed in order of appearance within the book, Professor Lisa Stein, of the American Associate Degree Early Childhood Educators; Teri Wallace, of the University of Minnesota; Cynthia Moreno Tuohy and Shirley Mikell, of the Association for Addiction Professionals, or NAADAC; Sue Casteel, of Gallaudet University; Meredith Bridges, of the National Recreation and Park Association; Reg Weaver, of the National Education Association; Chet Wichowski, of Temple University; Lorelle R. Swader, of the American Library Association; and Maria-Ortiz-Cordero, of New Mexico State University. Many others, working in related offices, deserve thanks for being so cordial and professional and for taking the time to make things happen. It's always easier to be too busy to help. Apologies go out to anyone whose name deserved to appear on this list but who was omitted by mistake.

The author also wishes to thank developmental editor Maura Christopher, who was a thoughtful presence throughout the process. And finally, thanks to her patient and supportive family. You are the best.

Introduction

Have you ever had a day when it's tough to get your act together? You know that kind of morning: You wake up slowly and can't figure out what to wear. You stand in front of the refrigerator trying to choose something to eat, but you draw a blank.

Many people feel the same way about planning their futures. Coming up with a career plan, and figuring out the "right" way to further your education, can be tough. It's understandable because this is not something you have practice with. Deciding what to do for a living is wide-open and unknown territory. It is normal to feel out of your element as you try to invent a happily-ever-after for yourself.

For years, your days have probably been planned out. You are told to attend elementary school, then middle school. You take high school classes with the idea of earning a diploma. Many people have a vague idea they will go to college but are undecided on a course of study. There are, certainly, those students who already know what they want to be; they have a map in their minds for how to get there. But they are a minority.

To make things tougher, your work experience is probably limited, so it can be difficult to appreciate the wide range of career options out there. If you're a teen, you may have taken part-time jobs: tutoring, bagging groceries, keeping basketball scores at recreation centers, working wherever your labor is welcome. But you are probably hoping to find some other employment for the long haul. So where do you start?

Career counselors say a fruitful search begins by thinking about the things you value. What activities are emotionally satisfying? Perhaps solving puzzles makes you feel really good. Maybe you feel your best when you're doing something artsy. When you have a list of what makes you happy, think about your skills. What are you good at? Maybe you're organized or are able to motivate others.

Identify your preferences when it comes to dealing with people. Perhaps you're happiest when surrounded by people. Maybe you like dealing with ideas instead! That's okay too. Write your thoughts down; then do some research. Let your school counselors help you; they have career-placement training. Use the Internet to your advantage; look up possibilities that interest you. Talk to people with attractive jobs. Find out if your ideas about the work match the day-to-day reality. Read books like this one, which aims to help you sort through available career paths.

This volume is part of a series dealing with careers. The chapters that follow feature high-demand jobs within the education and social services arena. Your prospects for finding employment within these areas are good—if you obtain the proper training. The National Center for Education Statistics crunched numbers and found that enrollment in elementary and secondary schools will be at record levels through 2014. More students means a greater need for educators and social service providers. This volume examines 10 careers in that sector.

Education and Social Services in Demand

The idea behind this series is to provide information that can help you imagine doing certain kinds of work. You might find that it's best to read the book cover to cover, feeling your way through and discovering which job sounds most like you. Or you can use the book for reference, by dipping into particular sections. You can look up a job title that interests you and read about the kind of coursework that is expected, the salary range, and more.

Many of the jobs profiled in this volume are ones that you may find in the schools you have attended; so you probably have some idea of the work involved. But the skills also translate to the private sector. All 10 are "people positions." They require skill with communication and with facilitating human interaction; so if you are the kind of person who can make people comfortable and figure out plans of action, you're looking in the right place.

Are you flexible? Creative? These jobs call for humor, goodwill, and resourcefulness. Is there a reservoir of patience within you? Perfect. Given that these jobs, from child care worker to vocational education instructor, focus on people, you can expect to deal with your share of the challenges that are tied to negotiating with human beings. There tends to be paperwork involved too; expect to be required to document the progress of the people in your care.

In this volume, you'll have a chance to consider the workday of a teacher assistant, a school administrative assistant, and more. The work of paraprofessionals like these, or people with two-year training, is fairly secure if current trends are any indication. "I think we've just continued to see that particular position over the past few years, over the past 50 years, continue to grow," says Teri Wallace, of the Institute on Community Integration, part of the College of Education and Human Development at the University of Minnesota.

First Things First

You do not need to wait for a degree to start you career path. Begin now to build support among professionals around you. Take advantage of relationships with school administrators, counselors, and teachers to find direction to explore careers in education and social services. People in these fields, especially those who chose to work with students, like to be helpful to others. Do not hesitate to ask questions of veteran teachers and social services workers.

The people working in these fields can probably tell you horror stories about their jobs, but they can also tell you that educating and providing social services for children and adults has built-in rewards. You help people realize their skills and potential. You leave a positive mark on individuals.

You can choose between helping children or adults—or strive to help both. In education, the advantage of teaching adults is that they take classes by choice. Disadvantages can include working at night, so your students can work during the day—and pay their tuition.

You can make a choice. But you will work indirectly with whole families in most of these jobs. Human services assistants and drug counselors (discussed in Chapters 10 and 3, respectively) most certainly deal with issues involving whole families. But preschool teachers and child care workers (Chapters 1 and 6), also featured, do as well. You might work in a traditional school setting or in a correctional institution. You could become a vocational instructor who teaches in corporations or a human services assistant who helps employees in a large firm. There is plenty of variety.

One of the best things about these careers is that, over a lifetime, you can move from one environment to another. A career is a path, after all. It winds through many landscapes.

Financial Future

The intrinsic rewards of working with people cannot be valued with dollars. But adults have rents and mortgages to pay, food to buy, and all the other practical considerations of life. When considering your future, you need to view the probable financial picture. Can you survive? More importantly, can you thrive?

The jobs detailed on these pages offer steady employment and earning opportunity. Almost without exception, you can gain experience and additional training and move into supervision, which pays more. And with an associate's degree, you start on much better footing than someone who ended his or her education after earning a high school diploma. Someone with a high school degree will earn $1.2 million throughout his or her working days, says the U.S. Census Bureau. But get this: A person with an associate's degree earns about $1.6 million in his or her lifetime, on average. Compared with those who hold only a high school degree, associate's-degree holders earn more money (that's an average $2,000 to $6,000 more per year) and face a much lower rate of unemployment.

Consider as well that 43 percent of four-year college grads are underemployed, which may mean taking a job at a fast-food chain when you have a degree in art history. Meanwhile, there's a much-bemoaned shortage of adults with technical skills who are needed for a wide range of work, from computer-chip technicians to child care workers. Many of the jobs reporting shortages can be attained with a two-year degree or related certification. "A four-year degree is a ticket to get in line for an oversold airplane," says Kenneth C. Gray, a professor of workforce education and development at Penn State University who thinks candidates often are better served by getting focused training in an area in which they would like to specialize.

Associate's Edge

All jobs considered in the series can be landed with an associate's degree. For many students, a four-year degree is financially out of reach. Many others are anxious to get on with adult life, so a decision to earn an associate's degree and enter the workforce sooner rather than later is proactive and practical. After all, you can decide later to go for additional training. For example, if you want to be a classroom teacher someday, you will need to pursue a bachelor's or perhaps even a master's degree. But, given that you already will have earned credits toward a bachelor's degree, it is hard to see a downside to pursuing a two-year diploma and working as a paraprofessional or related position.

In our computerized, fast-paced age, most managerial jobs continue to grow in complexity. This means that many tasks and responsibilities that were once the domain of education and social services grads with bachelor's and master's degrees are being given to those with certification or an associate's degree. "Some of the responsibilities, they're breaking them into bite-sized chunks," says Lorelle R. Swader, director of the American Library Association's Office of Human Resource Development and Recruitment.

Associate's degrees provide essential training without the expense of a four-year degree. More than 6.1 million students were enrolled in degree-granting two-year institutions in 2005, says the U.S. Department of Education's National Center for Education Statistics. The number of associate's degrees conferred continues to increase.

Some of the fastest growing jobs in education and social services—and many other major employment fields—require only associate's-degree training to start. The trick is zeroing in on the right ones. "It differs state by state. You need to know your state," says Professor Lisa Stein, of the American Associate Degree Early Childhood Educators. But prospects are good across all fields for associate's degree earners; experts in the early 2000s found that only 23 percent of 21st-century jobs require a four-year degree (www.bankrate.com/brm/news/pf/20020301a.asp). And do you know what else? Many jobs that require only a two-year degree, such as sign language interpreter, are considered safe in hard times.

Associate's degrees are not only available in traditional fields such as education, but in cutting-edge areas, such as computer animation and nanotechnology. The need for practical job skills is so great that high schools are tailoring curricula to develop skills needed to work in particular fields.

For instance, Palmdale High School, northeast of Los Angeles, opened the Health Careers Academy as a school within the school. Students graduate with health-occupation credentials and a chance to hold a good job in the medical field while in college. "These programs are intended to help prepare students for both college and work, not one or the other," writes Gary Hochlander of the Palmdale program and others like it in *The School Administrator*.

Flexibility has been and remains a main attraction of the two-year degree path. Classes are often offered at night, and many programs are taught on the Internet. You can work while you get your degree. Meanwhile, those looking for a traditional college experience will find that at least 20 percent of two-year colleges provide housing, cafeterias, sports, clubs, and an active social scene.

Many students find the two-year path especially fulfilling. Because associate's degree programs are occupation-oriented, students spend time getting hands-on experience. Real-world learning like this is often a prerequisite for landing an entry-level position. What's more, many internships and apprenticeships lead directly to full-time employment.

An Affordable Route

Statistics from the College Board show that the average annual total of tuition and fees for 2005–2006 at a four-year private college was $21,235, while the annual cost at a public two-year institution panned out at $2,191. What a difference that is! Plus there are multiple ways you can finance your training. Financial aid is not just for four-year college students—those attending trade, technical, vocational, two-year, and career colleges qualify too. Grant aid averages about $2,300 per student for those attending two-year public colleges, says the College Board. Schools that offer federal financing must be accredited, however, so be sure you check on that before you attend an institution. The U.S. Department of Education provides a list of accredited schools. You can look it up online at http://www.ope.ed .gov/accreditation/index.asp.

Just as with four-year students, two-year students who want aid usually must file the Free Application for Federal Student Aid (FAFSA). Lenders are increasingly helping the two-year student as well. SallieMae (see http://www.salliemae.com) offers private loans for career training, and U.S. Bank just introduced the CampUS Education Loan specifically for students who attend two-year schools.

Financing your education ends up like a puzzle. Different pieces fit in different corners. Just keep in mind that your two-year degree can be part of a long-term plan that includes further education, so your classes are like money in bank.

The Answer's in Your Hands

Plan your future logically: Prospects in certain fields look good. A two-year degree can get you where you need to go—and there are multiple ways to pay for related training. Earning a two-year degree will take you further than not having one, and you can tack on more education if need be. So what's to figure out except which field to study?

To zero in on a path, thumb through the material that follows. Remember that the selection of careers is by no means exhaustive. If you like what you read about a job, you might also consider the related careers listed at the end of each chapter. There might be something there for you to study further.

All lists, for schools with related two-year degrees or for associations that can provide connections, are meant as a starting point for your personalized job search. One thing leads to another.

Gaining admission to an associate's degree program is, moreover, not overly competitive. Students are admitted from a wide range of academic backgrounds. So someone who performed below average, for whatever reason, in high school can excel at a two-year school by putting in time and energy. You can make your second act count for more.

The most important things to consider about each position include the needed skills sets, education, and abilities, and its core values and future prospects. The more you know, the better you are able to make a decision about your probability of success as a paraprofessional teacher, library or recreation worker, interpreter, counselor, or administrator. With your own commitment, you have everything going for you.

Preschool Teacher

Vital Statistics

Salary: The median annual salary for preschool teachers is $20,980, according to 2006 data from the U.S. Bureau of Labor Statistics.

Employment: "Preschool teacher" ranks among the top 50 growth occupations. Employment opportunities are expected to move from good to excellent over the next decade. Growth is forecast to be faster than the average for all occupations through 2014, according to the Bureau of Labor Statistics.

Education: Your chances for employment are best if you have at least two years of education beyond high school. Most states require 12 credits of early childhood education or the completion of a two-year program in preschool or early childhood education.

Work Environment: Preschools are located in a wide variety of surroundings from houses to churches to schools. You will probably spend time outdoors as well, supervising the children's activity.

An early childhood educator encourages young children to grow through play, surrounded by caring teachers and comforted by an inspiring school setting. These educators provide opportunities to learn through games and both structured and unstructured activities. These teachers build children's vocabulary and language skills to help their students communicate in the larger world.

Now is a very good time to follow this career path. With a two-year degree in early childhood education, your job prospects are high, says Lisa Stein, president of the American Associate Degree Early Childhood Educators. "We do not have enough students with associate's degrees in early childhood education."

Beyond earning an associate's degree and continuing your education to take advantage of supervisory opportunities, you can enhance your job prospects in a couple of important ways. "The first is by being bilingual," Stein says. Preschool teachers who speak and write English and Spanish are in high demand. In addition, "We really need to see more multicultural representation in our workplace," she says. So if you have a unique background, it could become your asset as an educator.

The work is highly important. As a preschool teacher, you introduce early concepts of math, such as shapes and patterns. You help children develop their language skills by teaching sounds as well as the words for things, actions, colors, and ideas. You encourage understanding in science and social studies through the study of the natural world—plants, water, space—family, and community. To help children grasp the concepts, you use observation, easy experiments, games, activities, stories, art projects, computer applications, and other media. You encourage children to participate in the grand parade of life, rather than allowing the action to pass them by.

Some children are quiet and retiring; others never seem to stop talking or moving. In preschool, children begin forging their uniquely personal connections with other people and the world of ideas. Good preschool educators design their learning space to be colorful and crowded with books, games, and toys that encourage productive thinking.

As research shows, a child's early learning places him on the right track and helps determine his success in school. Preschool was a luxury not so long ago. But with fewer parents staying home, today more than 50 percent of children attend educational day care. As more children have been afforded early education, the expectations of the nation's kindergarten classes have been raised. It is no longer a miracle when a child can read a little before age 5, and with governmental pressure to standardize testing, a bit of systematic instruction is becoming a norm for the youngest students.

Philosophies of education differ, and trends in education come and go. But it is abundantly evident that preschool experience positively affects development. As a teacher, you maximize child-centered activities, making the most of classroom interactions. You can, if you are in tune, feel the excitement of the students' daily accomplishments immediately upon entering the classroom. At the best preschool centers, it is like walking into an enormous gift box filled with human potential and caring.

On the Job

As a preschool teacher, you stimulate curiosity and imagination by providing children with opportunities to learn. You don't just talk about how a store is run; you set up a play store and help the children "try on" the roles of the people who work there. You encourage questioning, observation, and experimentation. You ask students what they know about seeds, and then you help them grow some in cups and then you ask again. You treat your children with patience and care, knowing that they need careful cultivating, just like seedlings as they grow.

You'll teach kids with many brothers and sisters as well as only children. You'll have students who spend part of the week with one parent and another part of the week with another. You'll have clingy children and even some clingy parents, and you'll deal with both with respect. Some kids will live below the poverty line. Others have an abundance of consumer goods.

Each child arrives with a different package of skills. Some can name all their colors and shapes. Some can control a ball with ease. But some cannot cut with scissors or jump evenly. As a trained teacher, you recognize that language, social, and physical skills develop at different rates. You make contact with caregivers to understand outside influences. You keep track of each child's progress. You help new students, who arrive throughout the year, join in and enjoy themselves.

Your job is to create a program that celebrates and makes of the most of the diversity within your classroom. You play counting games, read aloud, and tell nursery rhymes and fairy tales. You model correct grammar and enrich vocabulary. Somehow, you do all this and allow plenty of resting and playing, along with lots of routine to make your kids feel in control and at ease.

> ## "I like a teacher who gives you something to take home to think about besides homework."
> ### —Lily Tomlin, comedian, as preschool character "Edith Ann"

🔑 Keys to Success

To be a successful preschool teacher you should have
- ⚷ a passion for working with young children
- ⚷ the ability to communicate with adults and little kids
- ⚷ great energy and enthusiasm
- ⚷ patience, compassion, and a sense of fairness
- ⚷ a knack for helping children grasp concepts
- ⚷ an understanding of the way young children learn

Do You Have What It Takes?

To succeed, patience is key. Sensitivity to cultural differences is also critical in diverse classrooms, which are the norm. You absolutely need a high energy level. Can you motivate kids to step outside of their individual concerns and work cooperatively? You need to show them that group efforts are productive and often fun, even though kids at this age are "me" centered. Creative thinking and organizational skills will go a long way in your efforts. But your work with your children is not your only concern. You also have to communicate well with coworkers and parents to create an atmosphere of optimum trust and learning.

A Typical Day at Work

Young children learn quickly through play and creative activities directed by teachers and aides. So your typical day is about fun—with purpose. Some programs are half days; others follow public school hours; others start at 6 a.m. and end when all caregivers have arrived, often as late as 6 p.m. The exact hours can vary, but as soon as the children arrive, you are "on." Today, Roger is the first one through the door, greeting you quickly in his rush to get started. It is already halfway through the year, so he runs to his cubby with confidence and puts away his coat and bag. You talk with his mom about a picture he made of his neighborhood—and how detailed it is. Roger overhears and begins to beam. He is anxious, however, to return to what he calls "the cowboy corner," and before you know it he has whipped over to the dress-up area and forgotten about the picture. Alicia, Em, and Talia arrive; they are in a carpool. Em has birthday snacks she insisted upon carrying herself. But she has run out of steam and needs your help. Talia checks the board and announces that it is a "blue day," then goes to water the plants on the windowsill. She knows her morning job by color.

How to Break In

If you are interested in this emotionally sustaining career, you should acquire practical experience working with young children as soon as possible. You can take part-time paid work with recreation programs, schools, and possibly even day care centers while in high school. A potential preschool teacher can also demonstrate the ability to help young children thrive through related volunteer work, such as reading aloud to young children in a local library. During your training for your associate's degree in early childhood education, you should be given a supervised student teacher experience in a preschool. Make the most of it. Join related groups like the National Association for the Education of Young Children and attend conferences and meetings to make contacts. Knowing other teachers or the parents of preschool-age children can be useful when searching for work.

Two-Year Training

Many community colleges offer a two-year degree or certificate, typically a Child Development Associate (CDA) certificate. The more education you have, the better your chances of landing better jobs. Usually, you will take courses in literacy and early childhood education. Subjects covered typically include health, safety, and nutrition and childhood development. You will learn about childhood development and communication. The coursework prepares graduates to work as preschool teachers in public as well as private or community-run preschools. You should earn field experience working and observing in a preschool. You study child development to learn to create a daily routine and learning environment suitable for young children. You train in a preschool under the supervision of a teacher and a college instructor. After your fieldwork, you return to the college classroom to share your experiences and learn from other students.

What to Look For in a School

When considering a two-year school, be sure to ask questions such as the following:

☞ Does the school grant a Child Development Associate (CDA) credential or equivalent certificate?

☞ Will I be prepared for preschool management?

☞ Does the program include enough of both principles of child care and its practices?

☞ What is the record of the school's placement office?

☞ Have the teachers had experience with preschool-age children?

☞ How available are the teachers for guidance?

The Future

Employment opportunities for preschool teachers differ depending on where you live, but jobs are expected to grow nearly everywhere at an above-average rate. The fast-growing states of California, Idaho, Hawaii, Alaska, Utah, and New Mexico will likely experience the largest job increases. Jobs are sure to be more readily available in inner cities and rural areas as well. The fact that preschool teachers frequently move into positions as supervisors will lead to some of the openings. Often people start as an aide and upon gaining experience, move to a position as teacher and then to lead teacher, with additional college training. Meanwhile, older preschool teachers continue to retire. This creates a steady stream of new openings.

Did You Know?

A majority of kids—65 percent—say that by the time they were 7 they had once had an imaginary friend.

Interview with a Professional:
Q&A
Susan Schapiro
Preschool teacher, Oceanside, New York

Q: *How did you get started?*

A: I knew I wanted to be a teacher since I was a kid. I always watched my teachers and knew I wanted to do that. I went to Brooklyn College and did education credits and then did student teaching through a very nice program called apprentice teaching. My senior year, I did nothing except be in a classroom and then do a methods class. That was nice, since I got more classroom experience than a normal student teacher.

Q: *What's a typical day like?*

A: My typical day was a little different, since I had a gifted class. There was more instructional work and less play, but I had to make the kids feel they were learning and playing at the same time. Emotionally, they were five years old, but intellectually, they were far ahead.

Q: *What's your advice for those starting this career?*

A: You have to love kids. Don't go into this unless you love kids! You have to understand, you can't do a lot of the things you might want to do because of the red tape—especially nowadays. I had the ability to have a bit more creativity, but nowadays I think that teachers are controlled more by the [New York] Department of Education. You also have to understand there are a lot of rules and paperwork, and your day ends much later than 3 o'clock.

Q: *What's the best part of the job?*

A: The kids are the best part of the job, really—because they're great. If you go into it because you love kids, then the best part of the job is what you're giving to them and getting back from them.

Job Seeking Tips

Follow these specific tips for the career of preschool teacher and be sure to turn to Appendix A for help with résumés and interviewing.

✔ Meet with the career placement office at your school.

✔ Talk to preschool administrators, teachers, and parents in preschool centers for contacts and career advice.

✔ Put together a portfolio of lesson plans or a résumé outlining your previous work with young children.

✔ Collect letters of recommendation from those who supervised you in related volunteer and paid experiences.

Career Connections

For further information, contact the following organizations.

American Associate Degree Early Childhood Educators
http://www.accessece.org

National Association for the Education of Young Children
http://www.naeyc.org

National Childcare Information Center http://www.nccic.org

Council for Professional Recognition http://www.cdacouncil.org

Pre[K]Now http://www.preknow.org

Associate's Degree Programs

Search the Web for the many schools offering related training. Here are a few to get you started:

Cincinnati State Technical College, Cincinnati, Ohio

Dean College, Franklin, Massachusetts

Southwest Florida College, Fort Myers, Florida

SMU Pre-School Teacher Training, Dallas, Texas

Financial Aid

Go to Appendix B for tips on securing aid. Here are a few scholarships or aid packages related to preschool education. Search the Web for more.

Bright Horizons http://www.brighthorizons.com/scholarship

Highland Community College http://www.highland.cc.il.us/admissions/scholarships.asp

StraightForward Media Teacher Scholarship
http://www.straight]forwardmedia.com/education

U.S. Department of Health and Human Services
http://www.nccic.org/poptopics/financialassist.html

Related Careers

Child psychologist, kindergarten teacher, bilingual teacher, library aide, preschool aide, recreation worker, special education teacher, teacher aide, and tutor.

Teacher
Assistant

Vital Statistics

Salary: Teacher assistants earn a median $19,400 a year, with about one-third of assistants represented by a union, according to 2006 data from the U.S. Bureau of Labor Statistics.

Employment: Employment is expected to grow at a rate at least equal to the average for all other occupations through 2014, according to the Bureau of Labor Statistics. Schools face an increasing need for paraprofessionals in special education as well as regular classrooms.

Education: An associate's degree in childhood education, combined with experience working with children, increases employment opportunities.

Work Environment: Paraprofessionals work mostly indoors in a classroom or "float" among classrooms. Some time may be spent outdoors with students during recreation periods.

On a message board for the National Resource Center for Paraprofessionals, paraprofessionals across the nation have an ongoing conversation about classroom issues. One person is looking for ideas on how to handle an unruly second grader. Another is trying to figure out what further certification is needed to be employed in another state. Then there is the question from "B."

"How did you guys get started? As I said, I am working part-time right now, I also spend about five hours each week volunteering in my kids' classes. I really love being in the classroom, and I am very much interested in special education. Thanks for your help, B."

Be like "B." If you are considering the role of a classroom paraprofessional, talk with people who do the work. This community of educational helpers is on the front lines of public and private education, handling students and shifting job expectations. They can tell you what is wonderful about the work—and what makes them crazed. On one hand, you're dealing with increasing class sizes, changes in teaching methods and technology, and additional record keeping and testing demands, just as the teachers are. But there are big pluses: With increased demands on the teachers' time, more paraprofessionals are needed. Employment is secure for the foreseeable future.

"I think we've seen that particular position, over the past few years, over the past 50 years, continue to grow," says Teri Wallace, of the University of Minnesota's Institute on Community Integration. "When education

funding decreases we often see teaching positions decrease and paraprofessional positions stay the same or increase."

Other pluses: The kids and teachers enjoy your company and your help.
Your work is appreciated, and no day is the same. People who like to help
people find this work engaging, despite—and sometimes because of—the
obstacles.

You could be working in a residential program or a preschool, in a private or public setting, helping musical geniuses or kids with behavioral
issues or both. Under supervision, preschool and elementary paraprofessionals often work with individual students in small groups. You
might listen to one student read or help a group put together a report on
the presidents. You provide individual attention by reinforcing the lesson
or helping students organize work. With specialized training, you may
work with students with physical or mental handicaps, such as limited
hearing. Bilingual aides help students navigate English.

Paraprofessionals keep elementary classrooms going, recording grades,
setting up equipment, and handing out supplies. You might handle routine
tasks such as checking homework, running off worksheets, and keeping attendance records. You might act as the go-to person for the A-V equipment.
Then you may supervise students during lunch and recreation periods,
stepping in with a little adult wisdom as needed.

In secondary school, you work with teachers of specific subjects, such as
chemistry. The tasks relate to the class, such as working on biology research
projects, helping students get organized for a big research paper in English,
or giving make-up tests in world history. If something has to be learned or
completed, you are there, offering encouragement.

On the Job

Feeling energetic? If you plan to work in elementary schools, you need to
keep up with active youngsters. You tower over your charges and will find
yourself standing, kneeling, and then standing again, in order to better
communicate with the kids.

Most paraprofessionals work mainly indoors but often are also responsible for outside supervision. So don't expect to stay locked inside all the
time. You are in demand on the playground, in the hallways, and on field
trips away from the school. Your day switches, often dramatically, from one
activity to another.

In elementary and secondary schools, aides who are bilingual (a real
plus for employment these days) may be asked to work with students and
parents whose primary language is not English. You will work closely with
people from all levels of the school hierarchy, so it is important to be able
to communicate well. In addition to working with the students and teachers, paraprofessionals often interact with administrators and parents. You

become familiar with school-wide educational methods and procedures, and you act as a representative of the school.

Often, throughout the day, you switch gears and take on supplemental duties, such as operating overhead projectors. Many schools have computers in the classroom or in labs, and assistants are often asked to help students use computers and software. You may also keep records of attendance, grades, and more.

In general, you get to do much of what the teacher does, but without bearing the burden of final responsibility for the classroom. With this breathing room comes the freedom it sometimes takes to make a positive difference in an individual student's educational experience. Caring paraprofessionals will find their circles widening each year, as they help yet another group of students advance toward graduation.

> **"Good teaching is one-fourth preparation and three-fourths pure theatre."**
> —Gail Godwin, author

Keys to Success

To be a successful paraprofessional, you need to have strong
- interest in children
- clerical know-how
- ability to communicate with adults and children
- energy and enthusiasm
- level of patience and awareness

Do You Have What It Takes?

Students who are interested in this career should enjoy working with children and be able to handle classroom situations with fairness and patience. The job requires good health and plenty of energy. A paraprofessional must be sensitive to the needs and feelings of students—and adults.

The ability to communicate and work well with coworkers in the classroom and the school are important for success. Paraprofessionals work closely with classroom teachers and must be good communicators and listeners. They have to be diplomats who know when to take direction and when to take charge.

A Typical Day at Work

If you work in a middle school, your day might begin with a quick meeting with the classroom teacher. You devise a strategy to get a group that was in a chorus meeting yesterday up to speed with a long-term project about city planning. You gather the needed materials so the teacher can make a few phone calls. Then you go together to an administrative meeting, to talk about an upcoming cross-curricular project about South America. Once the students arrive, the busy work of the day begins.

In an elementary school, you might be responsible for meeting the bus and escorting students to the classroom, collecting homework and lunch money, taking attendance, and helping the children to settle in. You may then work with groups or individual students on book reports.

When midday rolls around, you might take students outdoors for their rec period and then supervise the lunchroom. At the end of the day, you might escort children back to the bus and then return to the classroom for cleanup and a discussion. The teacher invites you to share concerns: Matt finally stopped giving people little shoves when he thought no one was looking. Abby still seems tired after her long illness.

How to Break In

While working on an associate's degree in education, and even while in high school, you should acquire as much experience working with children as possible. A typical certificate and degree program will include fieldwork in a classroom. But as a potential paraprofessional, you should demonstrate an early interest by volunteering to work with kids. You can often help in after-school programs or read aloud to children in a local library. You could also gain experience through part-time paid work. Many people find employment in summer and after-school camps or running recreation classes. You could tutor for free or for fees. Most hiring is done in August, so be sure to engage the help of the people in your school's career placement office before then. You should also contact schools or districts directly.

Two-Year Training

The No Child Left Behind Act of 2001 mandates that U.S. paraprofessionals may help instruct students only if they have an associate's degree or two years of college, or have met "rigorous" state or local assessment. In Canada, special college courses are required for some positions, such as those helping special-needs children. Many community colleges offer related two-year degrees, preparing graduates for the classroom. Courses are designed to cover classroom management, child growth and development, techniques of child care, and more. You will get at least an introduction to special education and learn about the challenges of cultural differences in the classroom. You will get a smattering of math and humanities that you can build on with electives. Working in a middle or high school setting, you need knowledge of specific subjects, such as math or history. Computer skills are always a plus; a good program will cover computers in the classroom.

What to Look For in a School

When considering a two-year school, be sure to ask these kinds of questions:

☞ Does the school provide an internship for on-the-job experience?

☞ What is the record of the school's placement office?

☞ Do they teach basic teaching skills and methods?

☞ Does the degree cover elementary as well as secondary education?

☞ What and how recent are the professors' experience and credentials?

The Future

As the population continues to increase and additional special needs are identified, opportunities for paraprofessionals will grow in proportion, unless education budgets are drastically cut. Nearly 1.3 million paraprofessionals were employed in 2004; you can expect average growth in those numbers, given the political clout that now comes from broad-based education support. Teachers will continue to rely on paraprofessionals to provide the personal attention many children require. Private as well as public schools will continue to use paraprofessionals to supplement teachers, especially as school administrations and their districts strive to meet the needs of all their students, including those with special requirements. Other openings can be attributed to the fact that many paraprofessionals continue their education and move into positions as teachers. Others simply tire of the physical demands of the work.

Did You Know?

Elementary and secondary public school enrollment rose 22 percent between 1985 and 2005, according to the *Digest for Education Statistics*. The fastest growth was in pre-kindergarten through eighth grade; enrollment rose 24 percent, from 27.0 million to 33.5 million.

Interview with a Professional:
Q&A
Reva Fagan
Teacher aide, Boynton Beach, Florida

Q: *How did you get started?*

A: I originally had a different field, but I wanted to be around when my kids were in school and I wanted to be up when they were.

Q: *What's a typical day like?*

A: Busy. I was working for the most part with pre-K and kindergarten, who are four- and five-years-old. They have lots of energy, and I had to keep up with them!

Q: *What's your advice for those starting this career?*

A: I think it's very fulfilling, and it's wonderful to watch kids come at the beginning of the year, and by the end of the year, they've grown and learned so much, it's amazing.

Q: *What's the best part of the job?*

A: Watching the kids grow up. I was also lucky enough to work with wonderful teachers, and you watch them grow up, too. I worked with one who was a young girl when I started and I worked with her for 10 years and I saw her grow up, too.

Job Seeking Tips

Follow these tips for those hopeful of becoming a paraprofessional, and turn to Appendix A for general help with writing résumés and interviewing.

✔ Decide what age and grade level interests you the most.

✔ Meet with counselors in the career placement office at your school.

✔ Talk with teachers, principals, parents, and school volunteers about finding work.

✔ Pursue related part-time or volunteer experiences and prepare a portfolio that shows your duties and projects.

Career Connections

For further information, contact the following organizations.

American Federation of Teachers—Paraprofessional and School Related Personnel Division http://www.aft.org

Council for Exceptional Children http://www.cec.sped.org

National Association for the Education of Young Children http://www.naeyc.org/

National Education Association—Educational Support Personnel Division http://www.nea.org

National Resource Center for Paraprofessionals http://www.nrcpara.org

Associate's Degree Programs

Search online for schools offering classes for prospective paraprofessionals. To get started, you might look into these:

Bucks County Community College, Newton, Pennsylvania

Community College of Denver, Denver, Colorado

Manchester Community College, Manchester, Connecticut

Moraine Valley Community College, Palos Hills, Illinois

Financial Aid

A few related scholarships and financial programs are listed here. Search the Web for more. For additional information on aid for two-year students, turn to Appendix B.

American Federation of Teachers http://www.aft.org/teachers/jft/loanforgiveness.htm

Mississippi Assistant Teacher Scholarship Program http://www.mscode.com/free/statutes/37/106/0035.htm

North Carolina State Education Assistance Authority http://www.ncseaa.edu/TAS.htm

Related Careers

Administrative services assistant, bilingual assistant, early childhood assistant, library assistant, preschool assistant, special education assistant, and tutor.

Drug and Alcohol Abuse Counselor

Vital Statistics

Salary: Substance abuse counselors earn a median salary of $32,130, according to 2006 data from the U.S. Bureau of Labor Statistics.

Employment: Employment is expected to grow faster than the average for all occupations through 2014—with ample opportunities especially for those with experience—according to the Bureau of Labor Statistics.

Education: A license in alcohol and drug counseling (LADC) or a state certificate is required. Two-year schools offer an associate's degree that leads to certification in the field. Continuing education is needed both to advance and to stay licensed.

Work Environment: Addiction counselors work in public and private facilities, including correctional institutions and residential care. Counselors frequently work in the evening.

A recovering alcoholic or drug addict has taken the first step: entering a program to help him or her live without a chemical crutch. But there are so many steps that they must follow—and on any given day, the steps do not follow any particular order. Certainly, there are recovery programs that talk about steps. You can break the transformation back to health into parts, but every minute can be a challenge for a recovering individual, and all the research in the world has still not answered the most basic question: How do you get all addicts to stop drinking and drugging for good?

Recovery is a challenging field that needs its own kind of heroes. They know who they are. "If [you] have passion for this field, helping people with alcohol and drug abuse and addiction, then [you] need to follow that," says Cynthia Moreno Tuohy, executive director of NAADAC, which is now known as the Association for Addiction Professionals.

It is substance abuse and alcohol abuse counselors who step up to the plate, armed with empathy and education. Each day, they meet a never-ending crisis head on. Counselors support individuals, helping them to identify behaviors and problems related to addiction and making referrals as needed. The addict often has a social network built around drug or alcohol use, one from which it can be wrenching to break away. The addiction often masks psychological problems. Yet each addict is different. So counselors help individuals get over addiction-related problems and conduct programs to prevent addictions from occurring in the first place.

Drug and alcohol abuse counselors do their work in public scenarios, such as correctional institutions, halfway houses, social service agencies, and vocational centers. They work for private agencies too: camps, health care centers, residential care facilities. Some counselors are self-employed and work in private or group practice. In each of these settings, counselors play a similar role: They work with clients to help them understand why they are compelled to abuse chemical substances. They strive to help them change their behavior. They work with families to help them cope with the problems of addicted family members.

The counselors' goal is to enable their clients to live productive lives free of addictions—and to clear away the damage. The road to this result can be a long one, and the setbacks and stresses are hard on the counselors as well as clients. But, "people in this field make a difference everyday, and you can't find anything more rewarding," says Moreno Tuohy. You may not be able to address every problem an individual faces; many addicts have many layers of frustrations and instabilities. But in some cases, you save a man or woman from drowning in addiction. You save his or her family from loss.

> **"Because I'm an alcoholic and drug addict, because I spent my life running and drowning, I wish I knew (then) what I know now, thanks to my recovery program."**
> —Janice Dickinson, considered the first supermodel

Keys to Success

To be a successful drug and alcohol abuse counselor you should have

- the ability to work cooperatively with physicians, social workers, and family members
- a strong desire to help others
- the ability to communicate effectively
- respect for the privacy of your clients
- flexibility in building a work schedule

On the Job

Substance abuse counselors are professionals. Their job is to help people break addictions to prescription or illegal drugs or to alcohol and to help recovering abusers and addicts put their lives back together. Counselors do their work through one-on-one sessions with individuals and in group settings. These sessions help counselors identify the addict's behaviors and the problems that relate directly to chemical abuse and addiction. They encourage a full examination of the suffering so patients can fully understand and reject the destructive path they are on.

Drug and alcohol abuse counselors do not work alone. Much of their days are spent in meetings and in consultations over the phone. They consult with other professionals, social workers, doctors, police, other counselors, and the addict's family members for help in drawing up a plan for a patient's therapy and recovery. Then they refer clients for help that is available at other social service agencies, such as back-to-work programs.

Counselors conduct educational classes for the addict's family and write progress reports for courts and probation departments. They work in collaboration with physicians and other health care personnel to utilize community resources that can help patients resume life free from addiction. They help, in any way they can, to make health possible again.

Drug and alcohol abuse counselors are increasingly concerned with prevention as well. An important part of their work is to conduct programs for adults and young adults aimed at preventing addiction from occurring in the first place.

You may visit schools and programs for teens and preteens, or you may make yourself available at senior centers. Throughout your work, you respect and build upon the privacy of the clients who have entrusted you with their innermost thoughts, fears, and often-heartbreaking life stories.

A Typical Day at Work

Your morning might be spent counseling individuals. Today a former client is visiting you. He has been off drugs for more than a year, but he's back for encouragement and a possible job lead. At the end of the morning, you help lead a group session focusing on encouraging your clients to take responsibility for themselves. Attendance is good. You are feeling as though you have made some headway by the time lunch rolls around. But your afternoon is demanding and complicated. One client is beside herself because she's been dropped from the methadone treatment at her community center. You consult with other professionals and determine that a referral to a welfare office is in order. As this is happening, you hear that a client's children are without food; their mother is on the skids. You send a volunteer to the house, and make a call to the woman's caseworker to check up on the children. Next you prepare a talk you'll give that evening to a community group. When you get home, you throw off your shoes and sit down with a huge sigh. You are exhausted.

Do You Have What It Takes?

You need knowledge of the causes and treatments of addiction and a strong desire to help. You also need some immunity to setbacks, be it an abiding sense of your place in a larger picture or knowledge that you can make a difference.

Addicts need help day and night, so their counselors need physical and emotional energy. You must possess patience and persistence. Most abusers relapse. Many never shake their demons.

You may be minimally supervised, so you should be conscientious. At other times you are part of a team of law enforcement, medical, and social services personnel. So you must be a team player. And you are probably someone who is thoughtful of other people and has a compassionate core. Sincerity and integrity are essential traits for successful dependency counselors.

How to Break In

Education and practical training are key, says Shirley Mikell, deputy director of NAADAC. She recommends talking to the managers at local counseling centers. "A lot of treatment facilities will encourage high school students to attend in-house training to get exposure to the staff and to the career," she says. "There are six-hour events that might be offered on a weekend." Some government agencies require an exam in addition to certification, so be aware of the requirements you face. Try to volunteer in a drug prevention troupe or a city drug council to demonstrate your interest, or do peer counseling at your school. Take psychology and biology courses in high school, and make sure to focus on honing your oral communication skills. Seek an internship as part of postsecondary training if one or more are not included as part of your coursework.

Two-Year Training

Some schools and colleges offer associate's degrees in the field; others offer certificate programs for students who have earned an associate's in a related field or are working in counseling. But to break into the field, you must be licensed or certified in drug or alcohol abuse counseling. Many social service agencies require a bachelor's degree and professional experience, but an associate's degree and certification can get you started.

In related education, you take general classes in case planning and management, co-occurring disorders, counseling theories and techniques, human growth and development, and professional ethics. In addition to coursework, a good program should include a practicum: workshops and field training in a setting where alcohol and drug treatment counseling is provided.

What to Look For in a School

When considering a two-year school, be sure to ask these kinds of questions:

☞ Does the school offer a certificate or an associate's degree in drug or alcohol abuse counseling?

☞ Does the program include supervised fieldwork in a setting where treatment is provided?

☞ Are specialized classes, such as adolescent studies, available?

☞ Are the instructors experienced counselors?

☞ What is the record of the school's placement office?

☞ Will the school help me fulfill requirements in the state I choose for employment?

The Future

Demand for substance abuse counselors is expected to increase in coming years as a growing number of employee-assistance programs expand their plans to cover substance abuse treatment. The fact that this is a stressful job works for and against employees in this field. Most of the time your work will go unfinished; it is difficult to mark successes in the traditional sense. But high turnover means you'll find job openings. Advancement without a four-year degree is limited, however, so consider programs where your credits will transfer should you continue your education. Some employers provide training for newly hired counselors; others offer time off or provide help with tuition if it is needed to complete a bachelor's or graduate degree. You will have to participate in classes, personal studies, and workshops to maintain certification. With experience and advanced education, you can become a supervisor or an administrator.

Job Seeking Tips

Follow these specific tips for alcohol and drug abuse counselors, and turn to Appendix A for general help with résumés and interviewing.

✔ Decide which aspect of drug and alcohol counseling you prefer— for instance, counseling teens, prison offenders, etc.

✔ Contact your state employment offices for information about job opportunities.

✔ Make sure you have the needed certification to be hired.

✔ Meet with the career placement officer at your school.

✔ Build a résumé of related volunteer experience.

Interview with a Professional:
Q&A
Michael Geller
Drug and alcohol abuse counselor, Brooklyn, New York

Q: *How did you get started?*

A: I was the youngest teacher in my high school—I think I was 21. It was 1968, and all the kids were getting high—LSD and pot and hallucinogens—and the principal didn't know what to do. He looked around and he looked at me and he said, "I want you to figure this out." So I started reading, and I started learning what they did in other schools. I was still a teacher, but I wasn't in a classroom any more, I was doing drug counseling. It was actually the first full-time drug program in the New York City public schools, but they took my work and made it into the SPARK program, which is still around.

Q: *What's a typical day like?*

A: What you're trying to do is to let people know you're available. What good is it to have a program if no one knows you're there? So you make yourself available, you have cards and flyers and posters, and you hope people come around. So the first part is outreach. You also see the people who come to see you, of course. You also go around to various referral sites. One thing you need to understand is what you can do and what you can't do. If there's something you need to do and you can't, you make a referral to a program that can do it.

You also have to keep good records, because you're in between a bunch of things. For instance, there's the city's Sunshine Law, which says your books have to be open and publicly available. There's also federal law, which states that drug programs receiving money from the federal government need to be confidential. In addition, you know that you can see the client for a very short period of time, and so it's helpful to talk to parents and relatives, the people in his or her life who are going [to stay].

Record keeping is also key because you want to know that progress is being achieved. One way we work is by giving the client positive alternatives to drug abuse. Another way is by building decision-making skills. When the pipe is being passed around, how do you turn it down? Thirdly, we give information, honest information, since if you give false information you destroy your credibility, and fourth, as I said, is referrals.

Q: *What's your advice for those starting this career?*

A: Well, there are programs now being run so people getting involved in substance-abuse prevention can get certified and licensed. Most states have certification and licensing programs, and you take tests to get certified— [the certificate is] called CASAC, for Certified Alcohol and Substance Abuse Counselor, and it's recognized between states. General salaries are from $30,000 to $70,000, and supervisors make much more. Find out if your state has a certification program. They often take life experience as credits, and you don't need a B.A. [bachelor's] or master's degree to get certifed.

Q: *What's the best part of the job?*

A: The really best part of the job is when you have dealt with a young kid or teenager and he or she was in bad trouble, and then you see him or her on the street or in the mall and they've got a baby carriage and another kid behind him or her and a smile on their face and you figure somewhere you must have done something right.

Did You Know?

More than two out of three jail inmates in the United States—68 percent— met the criteria for substance abuse or dependence in the year before their incarceration (U.S. Bureau of Justice Statistics, 2002).

Career Connections

For further information, contact the following organizations.

American Counseling Association http://www.counseling.org/am/ template.cfm?section+home

Counsel for Accreditation of Counseling and Related Educational Programs http://www.cacrep.org

The Association for Addiction Professionals http://www.naadac.org

National Institute on Alcohol Abuse and Addiction http://www.niaaa.nih.gov

National Institute on Drug Abuse http://www.nida.nih.gov/ NIDAHome.html

National Board for Certified Counselors http://www.nbcc.org

Associate's Degree Programs

Search the Web for some of the many colleges that offer associate's degrees or certificate programs in drug and alcohol abuse counseling. Here are a few to get you started:

Central Community College, Grand Island, Nebraska

Daytona Beach Community College, Daytona Beach, Florida

Hawaii Community College, Hilo, Hawaii

University of Utah College of Social Work, Salt Lake City, Utah

Financial Aid

Be sure to check out Appendix B for information on securing financial aid. Search the Web for related scholarships. Here are several related ones:

Outreach Training Institute
http://www.asapnys.org/Jobs/Free%20trainingm.html

National Rural Institute on Alcohol and Drug Abuse
http://www.uwstout.edu/outreach/conf/nri/nri_scholar.htm

St. Vincent De Paul Substance Abuse and Prevention Grant
http://www.spcollege.edu/Central/ssfa/GrantsPage/stvindepaul.htm#

Tylenol Brand Scholarship Fund
http://www.scholarship.tylenol.com

Related Careers

Clergy, counselor, human services assistant, labor relations specialist, legal aide, nurse's aide, occupational therapist, social worker, and teacher assistant.

Sign Language Interpreter

Vital Statistics

Salary: Full-time sign language interpreters earn almost $34,000 a year; if highly skilled, the median is around $57,000, according to 2006 figures from the U.S. Bureau of Labor Statistics.

Employment: You can expect employment gains among interpreters to be increase faster than the average for other professions. One reason: Employers must comply with the Americans with Disabilities Act of 1990, which, among its guidelines, requires public and private services to provide interpretations for members of the deaf community.

Education: To work in this country, study American Sign Language for two years and more. Become certified by the Registry of Interpreters (RID). Consider qualifying for the numerous levels and specialties, such as signing for legal situations.

Work Environment: The majority of interpreters work in schools. Others work in fields such as criminal justice, medicine, or theater.

Most people communicate with others all day, every day. You rely on being understood and on understanding one another. But communication among those who are deaf and those who can hear and speak is problematic without skilled interpreters. You can gesture, certainly, but gestures only go so far.

Just one person in 1,000 is deaf, but interpreters are in high demand because there are not enough of them to go around. You can enter this gratifying field with two-year training, though you will want to continue your studies; you need to practice to improve. "It's a Catch-22," says Sue Casteel, a recruiter for Gallaudet University in Washington, D.C. "You're not really ready [with two-year training], but you really need to throw yourself into the work."

You're learning a whole language, after all. American Sign Language (or ASL) is used by a majority of the deaf community in the United States and Canada. It is made up of hand and body movements and facial expressions, each with specific meaning. The words of sign stand for things, as do words in Japanese, instead of spelling sounds out, as in English. These signed words are layered for meaning.

Like spoken languages, there are regional differences in sign. So while ASL works in the United States, it will not get you heard in Brazil. But one fact is universal with sign languages: As discussion heats up, so do the actions.

To show spoken words as signs, you need to represent meaning as accurately and quickly as possible. Sign language interpreters do not just translate concepts. They try to capture the feelings and attitudes the speakers are trying to convey. They pay strict attention to words and inflections and try to represent intent as well.

Interpreters also pay close attention to the deaf and speak out for them, translating appropriate messages to a hearing audience. Ethics and emotional intelligence are crucial. You must maintain respect for the privacy of those for whom you work. You are responsible for forwarding articulate communications of universal and very personal nature. (Just think if conversations with your friends were broadcast!)

The 1990 Americans with Disabilities Act ruled that public and private services must be accessible to all. The act has benefited deaf, deaf-blind, and hard-of-hearing people, for whom a basic act such as shopping at a mall was sometimes quite difficult, and for whom finding employment was often impossible. As a result, interpreters are in demand as never before.

"As for regular employment: definitely! There is so much work available," says Casteel. "We're always searching for interpreters."

Just know what you're getting into. As you can imagine, the work can be very taxing. All of your mental and most of your physical powers are called into use. But interpretation is a crucial job, providing untold personal rewards. Every day has real meaning—for you and for the people you help.

On the Job

In a school, sign language interpreters shadow deaf or hard of hearing students throughout a day of classes and activities. They interpret lectures, discussions, and announcements. Sometimes you have to interpret private conversations with teachers and instructors—even fellow students.

In the private sector, sign language interpreters work where they are needed to meet the needs of a wide range of clients. You might be needed in a law office to interpret legal issues between a lawyer and someone seeking damages for a car accident; a courtroom to interpret the proceedings of a criminal trial; a medical office to facilitate doctor/patient communication before surgery; a government agency to help a deaf person navigate through the paperwork and steps needed to remodel a house.

Interpreters are much needed in the arts. There you bring arts enjoyment and culture to the deaf community by interpreting live performances. In a theater, an interpreter becomes the ears of a deaf audience member by translating the words and lyrics of a production. You show the show! Interpreters sometimes even "rehearse," along with cast members, before an actual production so that they are familiar with the action that is to come, to help make certain deaf audience members do not miss anything.

Some assignments take a lot out of you. After 20 minutes of interpreting, the ability to process messages and interpret them correctly is diminished, so sometimes you will work with another interpreter as a tag team. The repetitive motions can really get to you after a while. In fact, over 60 percent of interpreters have needed medical attention for related injuries. But you gain plenty personally. You convey a world of emotion and meaning and help a special subset of people make the most of life. What could be more rewarding?

"Sign language is so expressive. It uses body movement."
—Patty Duke, actress who played Helen Keller in *The Miracle Worker*

🔑 Keys to Success

To be a successful sign language interpreter you should have
- ☛ fluency in both English and American Sign Language
- ☛ an educated awareness of the issues important to the deaf community
- ☛ confidence in your public speaking skills
- ☛ the ability to interpret the words of a person to others
- ☛ flexibility to assist various types of clients

Do You Have What It Takes?

Many people will depend on you to fulfill an important need—communication. You must be able to work under pressure with ease. Speakers and sign language users will be relying on you for speed, accuracy, and objectivity. To manage, you will need sensitivity and understanding. You must demonstrate versatility and flexibility and be comfortable working with people of all ages—from the school child who needs you on a field trip to the psychologist who calls you into a mental health facility. Certain jobs will require your knowledge of technical language, such as medical terms. To interpret in television or live theater, you will have to adjust to a fast and animated pace.

How to Break In

The most important step in becoming an interpreter is training in American Sign Language and obtaining National Interpreter Certification. You need not wait for college to begin classes. Most interpreters train for two to five years and then continue to expand skills on the job and in continuing education. Find an area of interpreting that interests you. Are you interested in legal work? Medical? Do you crave the variety that a freelancer enjoys? While in training, make and maintain contacts with sign language users you come to know in your studies. Try to find part-time or volunteer work that brings you in contact with members of the deaf community. Look for opportunities to volunteer, such as in schools and at community centers.

A Typical Day at Work

You have signed up to work as a freelancer for an agency that provides interpreters on call. Yesterday you were subbing for a high-school student's translator during a meeting with the guidance counselor about college possibilities. You ended up chatting with the student afterward; she was trying to decide how to tell her parents that their first-choice university is not hers. Today, you are on your way to the airport. You will be accompanying a young deaf businessman to a conference, where you will be given your own room and some time in the evening to take in the sights. You are thinking this will be a nice change of pace. Meanwhile, as you sit on the train that is carrying you to the airport, you are scanning a book about video game-making. The young man's business is video-game design, in which his acute observation skills are valued, and you will be at a conference in which new games are being introduced. It has been a while since you have flexed your thumbs on a video game, so you are catching up with advancements and cluing yourself in to concepts you might be asked to interpret.

Two-Year Training

Colleges, universities, and adult education programs offer classes in American Sign Language. You can also learn at vocational rehabilitation centers. Even some public schools offer instruction. But knowledge of sign language is not enough to prepare you for a job as an interpreter. A two-year associate's degree and certification are the best minimal qualifications. Many community and two-year colleges offer associate's degrees that lead to certification. Coursework includes liberal arts classes such as written communication, oral communication, linguistics, and business. Classes related to issues of interpretation will be part of the curriculum, such as the role of the interpreter and a historical overview of the profession. Most two-year schools include training in public speaking and language development. A good sign language interpreter's program will provide plenty of opportunities for practice to develop both speed and accuracy.

What to Look For in a School

When considering a two-year school, be sure to ask questions such as these:

☞ Does the school teach American Sign Language?

☞ Are the instructors experts in sign after having worked as interpreters?

☞ Is the school familiar with the needs of the deaf community?

☞ What is the record of graduates obtaining certification and job placement?

The Future

The employment outlook is very good due to the Americans with Disabilities Act, requiring businesses and employers to remove barriers that prevent people from participating in their services. If an interpreter is needed, one must be provided; so government agencies, medical and legal professions, religious organizations, and more are hiring interpreters. There is now a shortage of interpreters meeting business standards, which plays to your favor. Public and private schools are hiring sign language interpreters as well. Deaf students are mainstreamed to regular classrooms and are often assigned the services of an interpreter. People with cochlear implants (surgically implanted hearing devices) are helped in much the same way, so your skills transfer. Agencies that provide interpretation are major employers to consider as well. Such opportunities are best in cities.

Did You Know?

American Sign Language is the fourth most common language in the United States today.

Job Seeking Tips

You can follow these specific tips for becoming an interpreter, and you can turn to Appendix A for help with résumés and interviewing.

✔ Decide which area of interpreting most interests you.

✔ Seek advice from the professionals in the career placement office at your school.

✔ Talk to members of the deaf community, other interpreters, or sign language users for leads.

✔ Contact agencies and school systems, and apply directly to private firms and state and federal government agencies

Interview with a Professional:
Q&A
Maureen Bishop
Sign language interpreter, New York, New York

Q: *How did you get started?*

A: I always had an interest in sign language because my mother is deaf, although she doesn't know sign. I started studying sign language my freshman year in college, and my professors recommended me to the local interpreter services. I worked for them for 10 years before going freelance.

Q: *What's a typical day like?*

A: A typical day depends on where you are interpreting—school, hospital, courtroom, etc. You have to remember, being a sign language interpreter requires you to be "invisible" to other staff and/or students. You are only there to be the ears and voice of the individual you are assigned to. So a typical day can be pretty lonely, as you cannot fraternize with staff.

Q: *What's your advice for those starting this career?*

A: Start learning sign language early! A lot of schools offer sign language as an elective now. Also, learn both kinds of sign (yes, there are two). American Sign Language is the language deaf culture uses as a primary language. This language is like learning any other—it has its own grammar and everything. The other form of sign language to learn is Signed English. Signed English is in the same order as English—same grammar and everything— and is useful when you have to interpret English classes or something word-for-word.

Q: *What's the best part of the job?*

A: For me, it's very easy. You get to keep to yourself, and even though an individual is totally depending on you for information, it is a very low-stress job (if you are fluent!)

Career Connections

For further information, contact the following organizations.

American Sign Language Teachers Association http://www.aslta.org

American Speech-Language-Hearing Association http://www.asha .org/default.htm

American Translators Association http://www.atanet.org

Laurent Clerc National Deaf Education Center http://clerccenter .gallaudet.edu

National Association of the Deaf http://www.nad.org

Associate's Degree Programs

Here are a few schools offering programs for sign language interpreters. Search the Web for more:

Burlington County College, Pemberton, New Jersey

Georgia Perimeter College Interpreter Program, Merin, Georgia

Kirkwood Community College, Cedar Rapids, Iowa

Palomar Community College, San Marcos, California

Financial Aid

For opportunities to finance your education, check online, and look in Appendix B for additional information on aid. A few related scholarships and work-study programs are listed below.

Dawn Sign Press http://www.dawnsign.com/about/index.cfm?prid=30

Harper College http://www.harpercollege.edu/academ/aels_h/slip/ wolf.htm

Registry of Interpreters of the Deaf http://www.rid.org

Related Careers

Adult literacy teacher, bilingual teacher, court reporter, foreign language interpreter, guide, medical transcriptionist, and special education teacher.

Recreation Worker

Vital Statistics

Salary: The median annual salary of recreation workers is $19,320, according to 2006 figures from the U.S. Bureau of Labor Statistics.

Employment: Growth in jobs for recreation workers will keep pace with the growth in all occupations through 2014. Retiring baby boomers may be expected to support the industry, but employment also will be sensitive to state budget limitations. Opportunities are greater for part-time employees than for full-time ones.

Education: It is wise to earn at least an associate's degree in parks and recreation and related fields to become promotable. The National Recreation & Park Association has certification for individual jobs.

Work Environment: Most work is done outdoors in recreational parks, summer camps, and community centers. Supervisors spend more time indoors.

What does recreation mean to you? Some people like to play hoops. Others prefer the *click* of knitting needles and the satisfaction of seeing rows of stitches turn into something to wear. Some people bend like pretzels during yoga sessions, for the sheer satisfaction of feeling flexible. Others express themselves through sculpture or painting. It's all good.

Recreation can also mean a satisfying career. You can be a recreation worker, helping others make the most of their free time and health. "A career in the industry offers many diverse and exciting opportunities with the benefit of helping to impact lives and the quality of life in a community," says Meredith Bridgers, an information manager for the National Recreation and Park Association. "In public recreation alone, there are dozens of different positions available."

Though some recreation jobs are temporary or easily filled by part-time students, with education in the field, you can become a supervisor and make a long run of this highly satisfying line of work. Nearly every town and city has rec houses and fields dedicated to the pursuit of health and happiness.

Adults are spending more time and money on recreation than ever before. The baby boomers are reaching retirement, and though many of them work longer than their parents did, their sheer numbers are filling beaches and golf courses. A concern for the care of their health and fitness has been drilled into them from the start. When they have free time, they often use it on activities that interest them or are good for their physical and mental well-being.

Older adults are eager to stay active. Parents also want to see their children participate in well-planned activities that are safely run. This participation takes many forms—performing arts, camping, sports like swimming and tennis, team sports such as baseball and soccer. These activities take place regularly in social settings with the help of rec workers.

You might be coaching middle school basketball, setting up the scoreboards for high school soccer tournaments, slowing down the pitching machine when the little kids step up to plate. It's the kind of job in which you are often known by first name. You're the one with the whistle, the smile, the helping hand. You might handle administrative duties or take care of grounds as well.

Recreation workers plan, organize, and direct activities on ball fields and in recreation areas, parks, nursing homes, and community centers. Some work in summer camps in the country; others oversee urban playgrounds. They pass on important concepts like cooperation and fair play to young children; they encourage talent in people of all ages; they make it possible for visitors to senior centers to work together on a daily basis. They teach crafts, dance, and drama; they organize sporting events; they supervise playgrounds and pools. A job as a recreation worker is a great one for someone who enjoys leading an active life, working with people of all ages and all ability levels, and who thrives on variety.

On the Job

People arrive at community or rec centers hoping to learn a new sport, perfect a skill, or work with others on a group project. Rec workers make this possible by planning activities, gathering materials, and planning to ensure everything goes right. As people say, "It's always something!" You might spend almost all day outside, supervising youth-league baseball or teaching swimming. Or you might be indoors, leading classes in dance, drama, or crafts. If you are a recreation worker at a small center that serves a varied population of older adults, preschoolers, and after-school groups, you become adept at working with all kinds of people. In a camp or large facility, you specialize and teach only basketball or only preschoolers.

Whatever, whenever, there is one thing you need to be: flexible. The main ingredient of any activity is people, and they can be unpredictable. Success in this line of work comes from your empathy and from knowing that every group activity requires a unique set of skills from you and your charges and different safety and social rules. The senior citizens who toss a giant ball to one another in a circle are accomplishing one thing. The wired three-year-olds who attempt to lift a parachute on cue are doing something else again. An educated rec worker doesn't just go through the motions. He or she is aware of what can go wrong—and right. A gym class for troubled teens, a sports team that includes an autistic child, an overcrowded preschool dance class, or an adult exercise group that includes people with a wild variety of skill levels all present different challenges. You strive to make sure all participants feel successful. With experience and education, you can take on more supervising and do more planning. You manage the calendar, order supplies, register participants, make budgets, and organize special events. Mostly, you make people happy.

"Leisure is the time for doing something useful."
—Benjamin Franklin, statesman

🔑 Keys to Success

To be a successful recreation worker you should have
- 🔑 a talent for dealing with people of all ages
- 🔑 energy and enthusiasm
- 🔑 an outgoing and friendly nature
- 🔑 a flexible schedule
- 🔑 an interest or talent in a particular sport, craft, or skill

Do You Have What It Takes?

Are you outgoing? Good at motivating people? Talented in a skill, such as music, or a sport like swimming? If you answered yes, then you may have what it takes to succeed as a recreation worker. You will be in direct contact with participants from preschool aged to older adults. They look to you to plan and carry out activities that are suitable and fun. They expect you to be fair and friendly with everyone. You need to make sure everyone is participating at their comfort level and understand what is appropriate. Facilities are often open weekends and evenings. You need to be flexible with your time.

How to Break In

Volunteering at a grade school, taking a summer job as a camp counselor, or working with older adults at a center are all going to help you break into a job in recreation. Employers are looking for people with experience; so perfect your special skills—play the sports you enjoy, practice music, use your art talent. These and related skills will make you attractive to employers. Make sure that your certifications, such as life guarding or aerobics training, are current. Join related associations and keep up to date with safety regulations. At your community college, be sure to complete an internship. Later, stay in touch with your instructors and the people you met in your practical training. Make contacts at workshops and conferences.

A Typical Day at Work

At your community center, the hired workers are few, so you have many duties to cover. In the morning, you act as an arts facilitator. Your first group is mainly older adults, eager to learn photography. You discuss the basics of good composition and demonstrate the use of a digital camera. They especially enjoy taking photos of one another and loading them on the computers. Later in the morning, a group of preschoolers arrives with parents and caregivers. You conduct another art class, this time using giant pieces of paper and colored pencils and poster paint. The children lie on the paper and you outline them. Then they decorate the forms. You spend time making sure they understand the activity and that they work cooperatively. The paints you've selected—you're no dummy—wash out of clothing. In the afternoon you travel to a local park to organize outdoor stretching exercises for a group that includes senior citizens and moms with kids in strollers. Near the end of the day, you go back to the office to call the high school to arrange for volunteers for a senior citizen's outing, and you create a calendar for next week's classes.

Two-Year Training

Programs leading to an associate's or bachelor degree in parks and recreation or related fields are offered at many colleges, community colleges, and universities. An accredited program provides exposure to the history and theory of public recreation as well as more practical courses, such as motor training, physical fitness and flexibility, swimming, lifeguard certification, and aerobic conditioning. A good program should offer courses that teach community organization skills and administration methods, in addition to classes dealing with special populations, such as the elderly or people with disabilities. Supervised fieldwork should be available. Students interested in specializing should seek out courses in areas such as therapeutic recreation, park management, or camp management. The many aspects of recreation cover planning, the frontline staff, administration, and grounds and maintenance.

What to Look For in a School

When considering a two-year school, be sure to ask questions like these:

☞ Does the program include supervised fieldwork?

☞ What real-life experience do the instructors bring to the classroom?

☞ Is this a career-track program with classes in administration and management?

☞ Does the school concentrate only on sports or branch into classroom instruction?

☞ What is the record of the school's placement office?

☞ Is the school connected to related recreation associations?

The Future

Jobs in recreation are appealing on many levels and will continue to attract applicants. Those whose training includes practical experience and a two-year degree enter the field at an advantage. Competition for career-track positions, such as directors and assistant directors, will remain keen. These positions go to people with formal training and experience. The industry includes a large number of part-time, seasonal openings, mostly in the summer. You should aim to supervise the students and others who take these positions. Community budgets ebb and flow, affecting the number of paid positions available at any given time. But the American obsession with making the most of leisure time assures steady employment opportunities in recreation. The industry extends to hospitality and tourism as well. Look for other paid opportunities in private-sector enterprises, such as skating rinks and fitness clubs.

Did You Know?

Cruise ships and luxury liners employ recreation workers to work with the passengers on board. It can be a great way to travel and work at the same time.

Job Seeking Tips

Follow these specific tips for recreation workers and then turn to Appendix A for help on résumés and interviewing.

✔ Meet with the career placement office at your school.

✔ Talk to the directors of local community centers.

✔ Contact state, county, and city departments of parks and recreation.

✔ Attend workshops sponsored by sports and fitness organizations to keep your certification and skills up to date.

Interview with a Professional: Q&A

Lewis Perlmutter

Recreation worker, Oceanside, New York

Q: *How did you get started?*

A: I always wanted to be a teacher when I was younger, and I pursued it in college and got a job. My strengths were in discipline and organization, which led me to mass-group organization. You didn't need any special certification, or at least you didn't when I got into it, but I coached high school basketball and took all sorts of courses in CPR [cardiopulmonary resuscitation] and stuff.

Q: *What's a typical day like?*

A: I'd go in early, and I was like the jack-of-all-trades—scheduling, organization, programs—and then I would teach 2 or 3 gym classes and do 2 or 3 lunch duties.

Q: *What's your advice for those starting this career?*

A: First off, I would get into the high schools. Elementary school is fine, but you only teach basic organization and discipline and basic motor skills. In high school, you teach activities and sports, and it's a lot more rewarding.

Q: *What's the best part of the job?*

A: The satisfaction of seeing a kid grow and improve. And, of course, in seeing him or her really grow up. Not everyone's going to be an NBA player, but to see him go to college and make something of himself, that's really satisfying.

Career Connections

For information about jobs in recreation, contact employers such as local government departments of parks and recreation or local social or recreation organizations. The following organizations would be good places to start.

Canadian Parks and Recreation Association http://www.cpra.ca/

National Recreation and Park Association http://www.nrpa.org

Resort and Commercial Recreation Association http://www.r-c-r-a.org

Sport and Legal Recreation Law Association http://www.srlaweb.org

Associate's Degree Programs

Search online for schools offering recreation and leisure studies programs. To get you started, here are a few:

American College, Sacramento, California

Community College of Baltimore County, Dundalk, Maryland

Fond du Lac College, Cloquet, Minnesota

Lake Superior State University, Sault St. Marie, Michigan

Financial Aid

Here are a few related scholarships. Inquire about financial aid too. For more information, turn to Appendix B.

Illinois Park and Recreation Association http://www.il-ipra.org/ Affiliations/Foundation/Scholarships.cfm

Iowa Park and Recreation http://www.wku.edu/recreation/ scholarships.html

Western Kentucky Recreation http://www.wku.edu/recreation/ scholarships.html

Related Careers

Coach, conservationist, counselor, fitness instructor, lodging manager, meeting planner, museum technician, recreation therapist, teacher aide, teacher, tutor, and umpire.

Child Care Worker

Vital Statistics

Salary: The median hourly wage for child care workers is about $8, with the higher wrung of more-educated workers earning more than $12 an hour, or about $25,000 a year, according to 2006 figures from the U.S. Bureau of Labor Statistics.

Employment: Child care is a source of steady employment in the United States and will see growth through 2014 in line with other industries, according to the Bureau of Labor Statistics..

Education: Many states have a minimum educational or training requirement, such as a high school diploma or GED, a degree in early childhood education from a two-year school, or a CDA (Child Development Associate) credential from a child day care organization.

Work Environment: The majority of child care workers are employed by federally funded Head Start programs, nursery schools, or day care centers. Working hours vary.

Ask child care workers, world over, about their jobs, and you'll hear anecdotes about kids. "We observe the children and what they're interested in and set goals that relate to their interests," says Kaitiaki Tamariki, a nanny who posted her thoughts on a New Zealand government Web site. "For example, one of the boys I look after is really interested in water, and he finds a hundred ways to use it. We want to introduce words and letters to him now, but there's no use giving him a book because he's just not interested, so we put the letters into the water, and he plays with letters and the water together."

Tamariki is making a difference in that child's life. Brain researchers say you can look at someone's first few years and nearly predict his or her future. You can't know whether he or she will become a carpenter or a surgical equipment sales rep. You can't guess if he or she will be a good driver. But you have an idea how well a child will fare by knowing about the creative care he or she received initially.

During a child's first years, intellectual and social development is cast, like a die. Some researchers suggest that being home is best; others say time spent in child care, among peers, is better. But one thing is clear: the more caregivers offer, whether they are parents or hired hands, the better the next generation fares.

If a career in child care interests you, the pros say you should earn at least an associate's degree in early childhood education to maximize the potential of the children in your charge, along with your own. You want to be ready to take advantage of opportunities that present themselves. The employment picture is changing in early childhood. "It used to be that anyone could get a job," says Professor Lisa Stein, of American Associate Degree Early Childhood Educators. "But what we see federally with Head Start, which starts the trends, is that to be a lead teacher, you need that associate's degree."

Your education should underscore an innate interest in helping kids and families. Child care has far-reaching social and economic effects. Most parents now work outside the home. The percentage of moms in the workforce doubled from 1970 to 2000. All too often, extended family members who could help out with child care now live too far away. Child care workers are in demand, keeping children healthy and safe at day care centers, in nursery schools, within private homes, and at government facilities. For-profit sites operate independently or as part of a chain. Not-for-profit facilities are often connected with religious institutions, YMCAs, or other social and recreation centers, schools, or agencies. You can pick and choose your venue.

So what do you say? Are you someone who enjoys helping children deal with the world? Are you energetic and flexible, creative and fun? Each day, small children wake in anticipation of wonder. Just being around them is enjoyable. But helping them reach their potentials, showing them how to iron out problems . . . this can bring lasting joy.

On the Job

The care of children covers all kinds of acts of kindness and understanding. You serve healthy meals and snacks, supervise rest time, and adapt the daily routine to the needs of individual children whenever necessary and possible. Day by day, you are their rock.

Child care workers work to help children acquire new skills from infancy. Your time with the kids should be filled with opportunities to expand skills and understanding. Everything babies, toddlers, or youngsters do leads to their greater understanding and readiness to go out into the world. Everything!   Young children use games and physical activities to improve coordination and flexibility. Just hanging around other children helps advance their social skills. With the encouragement of skilled child care workers, kids develop tolerance and learn to cooperate with each other and with authority figures. Through activities such as art, music, play, and storytelling, they acquire skills that they will use in school when they are older.

The work can seem routine on the surface, but challenges define each day. You must be constantly alert, anticipate trouble, and avoid it. You must deal with disruptive children, keep the group busy, and be fair and firm with everyone.

The number and ages of the children under your care can vary widely. You have to adapt programs to account for these differences. When you notice a troubling situation, you must find a solution. Part of the job is thinking of ways to solve problems and developing guidelines that children can follow.

The hours for day care, nursery school, and similar programs can be long. Many centers open early and do not close until the last child has been picked up by parents. Emergencies and unexpected events can make them late. But the positives of the job are clear. It is a terrific job for people who like variety in their day, who are happy to be around children, and who pride themselves on their creativity and helpfulness.

> ## "If our American way of life fails the child, it fails us all."
> **—Pearl S. Buck, author and Nobel Prize winner**

Keys to Success

To be a successful child care worker you should have
- an interest in working with children
- a talent for communicating with children, parents, and coworkers
- patience and a sense of fairness
- energy and enthusiasm
- the ability to work as part of a team
- flexibility to adjust your schedule as needed

Do You Have What It Takes?

Are you creative and energetic? Do you enjoy being part of a team? Child care workers must be patient, supportive, and enthusiastic. Young children are constantly on the move, so it is important to have physical stamina. You'll find yourself bending, lifting, pushing, pulling, walking, and running on this job. Creativity plays an important role too. Young children have short attention spans that demand an inventive program of activities. Older children need age-appropriate care.

As a child care worker in a day care center, your team includes supervisors, children, parents, and other staff. Communication is paramount. You must be able to express ideas clearly to children and other adults.

A Typical Day at Work

As each child arrives, the door gives a familiar squeak. Ben is dragging. You give him some space, but resolve to ask him what's going on. A group of girls accosts you; they want to tell you about seeing another worker from the center when they stopped at a coffee shop on the way to school. You give one and all an upbeat greeting and help them settle in. Today you have set up a table with fruit cutouts, and you ask each child to pick a favorite and color it so you can be ready for a conversation about seeds later on.

Just before lunch, crankiness overtakes them. You make sure they eat decent food and get some rest, changing the diapers of the younger ones, cleaning up or helping them to clean up after themselves. You know it is important to keep surfaces—anything the children touch at the center—clean and free of germs.

Ben and Andrew are fighting. You jump in to encourage them to settle their differences with "inside voices." Kids feel a wide range of emotions that are often out of place. You deal with disruptive children regularly. And you see the bigger picture: the development and growth of the entire group.

How to Break In

You can demonstrate an early interest in child care through volunteer work, such as reading aloud to young children in a local library or helping out before or after school in a day care center. Take any classes your high school offers that cover child development. Consider making one or more of your long-term research projects in English or science or social studies relate to the field. Contacts, such as other child care workers or the parents of preschool-age children, can be useful. Continue this thread throughout your college career. Make contacts with people likely to refer you or employ you once you have your degree.

Employers look for people who enjoy working with infants and children. Babysitting experience is helpful. So is a second language, such as Spanish.

Two-Year Training

Many community colleges offer classes that prepare graduates to work in for-profit and not-for-profit day care centers. Their programs focus on the care, culture, development, and language of young children. An associate's degree or certificate in early childhood education provides an underpinning of both theoretical knowledge and practical skills. In your training, you will study child growth and development, general psychology, the use of computers in early childhood education, children's literature, curriculum development for young children, principles behind creative play and art, and more. You will also learn practical skills in caring for infants and young children. A good program will provide an overview of policies and procedures—and safety regulations. Most offer classes in nutrition and health and safety, in oral and written communication, and in health care, first aid, and fire safety. You will learn to recognize the often-specialized needs of children and families and address them. The more education you have, the better your chances for advancement.

What to Look For in a School

When considering a two-year school, be sure to ask questions like these:

☞ Does the school offer a degree or early childhood certification?

☞ Does the program include real-life experience with kids?

☞ Does it offer courses in nutrition, safety, and language development?

☞ What is the record of the school's placement office?

☞ Have the instructors worked recently in child care facilities?

☞ Does the school have an on-site child care facility or a relationship with local caregivers?

The Future

Job openings are expected to see average growth through 2014, and continuing your education can help you advance in this career. However, there are other factors to consider as you look forward. The National Association for the Education of Young Children unveiled a new accreditation system at their 2006 professional development conference. Educational programs are undergoing peer reviews, confirming that qualifications are met. It probably makes sense to see whether your educational program is planning to comply.

On the level of national trends, Head Start, a federally funded early child care program, saw its funds sharply reduced in 2006 just as states and localities nationwide were passing laws favoring increased pay for direct care workers as well as their right to organize. Regardless of federal funding trends, state and local efforts should further stabilize the workforce and help gain a collective voice to raise benefits and subsidies.

Did You Know?

Kids, kids, and more kids! The number of children under age five in the United States in 2005 was 20.3 million, according to the U.S. Census Bureau. About 67 percent of them are in child care.

Interview with a Professional:
Q&A
Courtney Desmond
Child care worker, Lowell, Massachusetts

Q: *How did you get started?*

A: I got started when I was a freshman in college. I was hired through a nanny agency, and I connected with a great family. Five years later, I work full-time independently for the same family, who pay me way more than I would make in the "real world" and they pay for my insurance.

Q: *What's a typical day like?*

A: On a typical day I get to work around 7 a.m. The parents leave, and I get the two older children ready for school. I put them on the school bus at 8:30, and I spend the rest of the day with a two-year-old. On Mondays and Wednesdays we have classes like music and swimming, depending on the season. The other days we just play or go for a walk to the park. At 1 o'clock she goes down for a nap, and I run the dishwasher, do some laundry, and then relax until I wake her up a little after three. At 3:30 [p.m.] we pick up the older kids from the bus stop, then we have snack and do homework or outside play or arts and crafts until Mom gets home at five.

Q: *What's your advice for those starting this career?*

A: My advice is in order to be a full-time nanny, you need a lot of patience, and you need to find the perfect family. I am lucky that my nannying style perfectly fits with the family's parenting style, but some of my nanny friends are not as lucky. Everyone needs to be on the same page for things like discipline, activities, and meals. If you are going to be a nanny, you also need to find a family that is willing to treat you like an employee rather than a babysitter. I get sick days, paid vacations, and insurance.

Q: *What's the best part of the job?*

A: The best part is the kids. They are fun, and I have a fun job. Also, my job is very flexible. If I don't feel like going outside, I just do an indoor activity with the kids. Also, I have at least two hours of relaxation every day when the baby is sleeping, which helps me keep my sanity on bad days.

Job Seeking Tips

Be sure to turn to Appendix A for general help with résumés and interviewing. Here are helpful tips for becoming a child care worker.

✔ Meet with the career placement office at your school.

✔ Talk to supervisors and staff at local day care centers, nursery schools, or Head Start programs.

✔ Put together a portfolio outlining your previous work, lesson plans, and activities with young children.

✔ Join organizations such as American Associate Degree Early Childhood Educators.

Career Connections

For further information, contact the following organizations.

American Associate Degree Early Childhood Educators
http://www.accessece.org/

Center for the Child Care Workforce http://www.ccw.org

Child Day Care Association
http://www.childcarestl.org/joom/index.php

Council for Professional Recognition http://www.cdacouncil.org

National Association for the Education of Young Children
http://www.naeyc.org

National Childcare Information Center
http://www.nccic.org

Associate's Degree Programs

Search online for schools offering associate's degree programs in early childhood education. To get started, look into these:

Blue Mountain Community College, Pendleton, Oregon

Denmark Technical Center, Denmark, South Carolina

Lake Michigan College, Benton Harbor, Michigan

Gateway Community College, New Haven, Connecticut

Financial Aid

For more information on financing your education, turn to Appendix B. A few of the many scholarships related to early childhood education are listed here to start your search.

Community College of Philadelphia http://www.ccp.edu/site/current/scholarships

Edmonds Community College http://scholarships.edcc.edu

Fred Rogers Memorial Scholarship http://www.emmys.org/
atemmys/rogers-scholarship.php

Metropolitan Washington Council of Governments
http://www.mwcog.org/services/human/hesp

T.E.A.C.H. Early Childhood Project
http://www.childcareservices.org/ps/teach.html

Related Careers

Babysitter, children's library assistant, infant care, nanny, preschool teacher,
recreation worker, teacher aide, teacher, and theater arts teacher.

School
Administrative
Assistant

Vital Statistics

Salary: The median salary for an administrative assistant in education is just over $26,000, according to 2006 figures from the U.S. Bureau of Labor Statistics.

Employment: As reliance on technology increases, the number of office positions is expected to grow more slowly than the average for all occupations through 2014, according to the Bureau of Labor Statistics; however, the role of a school administrative assistant is going to remain indispensable.

Education: Training in office skills from your high school business or vocational department is helpful; a two-year degree at a community college, a technical institution, or a business college is best.

Work Environment: School offices—in elementary and secondary schools, and in colleges—are usually friendly, busy environments.

Registrations. Bus schedules. Immunization requirements.

Parent communications. In any school, there is a mountain of detail work to be done, keeping track of students, teachers, administrators, and everyone's well-being. Schools are calling for good people who can conquer those mountains and smile while doing it—personable people with a knack for organization who can manage all the loose ends. They are looking for the next generation of school administrative assistants, the super secretaries. These are very vital jobs.

"In many institutions, it is the school secretary who runs the office," says Reg Weaver, president of the National Education Association (NEA). "The tone and the attitude exhibited by that school secretary is something that a parent or student can take with them. It can determine whether the relationship with the school is negative or positive."

The acts of daily kindness that school secretaries show students are just part of the work involved. Take the average number of times a year you needed help from the office and multiply the number of students in school, then add untold duties of a far-reaching range.

"When kids get into trouble, teachers send them to the principal's office, and the principal often isn't there. So who watches them? The school secretary!" says Weaver. "The secretary serves as another kind of parent, someone to provide guidance."

In the front offices of the approximately 14,000 U.S. school districts, meetings are planned and scheduled, appointments made, interviews conducted, official records kept, and district communications are conveyed. Although the responsibilities of an administrative assistant vary depending on the size of school, the time of year, and the age of the students, the skills needed to help run the office are similar everywhere. An administrative assistant operates and troubleshoots office equipment; coordinates activities; and fosters communication among administrators, parents, students, and teachers. It is the job of an administrative assistant to provide information to staff and to keep confidential and orderly records concerning students and teachers. He or she is the principal's right arm—often the person who enables the principal to be an effective administrator.

To know what the job is really like, ask people who have done it. They witness the history of their communities as families grow and pass through schools, as the days bring their unique challenges, one after another. "As a school secretary, I saw more and more students and families with financial and emotional challenges, as well as special circumstances," explains Karen Mahurin, president of the NEA National Council for Education Support Professionals on the NEA Web site, about her 22-year career at front desks. "They needed extra attention, and as a secretary and someone they knew and trusted, I was there to give it to them."

On the Job

Communication is job number one for a school administrative assistant. Not only do you need to be pleasant on days when you don't feel like doing so, you also have to have a keen understanding of how communication flows. You do not want to leave the wrong people out of the loop—or the right people either!

Everybody finds his or her way to the office: maintenance workers, students, principals, teachers, teacher assistants, and other school employees. In addition, parents and other administrators are frequent visitors to the school. The daily schedule of a school can seem like chaos to some people, but not to an organized person in the front office.

The people who just moved to the district want to know where to forward their school records. A seventh grader needs the permission form—for the third time!—that will allow him to try out for baseball. A grandmother walks in lost, called to bring home a sick child. The principal needs help organizing a meeting for the foreign language committee. You need to make sure that others who might be affected by the committee's decisions know what transpired. Meanwhile, you are ordering, tracking, storing, and distributing supplies. You are the office equipment czar, responsible for computers, copiers, fax machines, scanners, and video equipment. You might track attendance, fill stockrooms, and pay bills. Schools' buses and field-trip transportation also must run smoothly, and you may need to step in when they don't. If that seems like a lot of work—it is! But people who thrive in this kind of environment love it.

You are the gatekeeper. You probably know more than anyone about the school and how it runs. Everything you do benefits someone.

> ## "Nine tenths of education is encouragement."
> —Anatole France, Nobel Prize–winning author

🔑 Keys to Success

To be a successful administrative assistant in a school you should have

- 🔑 a keen ability to communicate
- 🔑 energy and enthusiasm
- 🔑 patience and the ability to keep cool under pressure
- 🔑 strong organizational abilities
- 🔑 excellent office skills and a familiarity with the newest software applications

Do You Have What It Takes?

Are you a friendly person? Do you enjoy handling a number of tasks at once? Does it give you satisfaction to keep things orderly and calm? Then you have what it takes to work as an administrative assistant in a school. You need to master basic office skills and knowledge of software applications, such as the Excel spreadsheet program from the Microsoft Office Suite. You should be fast and accurate on a keyboard. Your English and communications classes will come in helpful, as will a second language. As an administrative assistant, you are part of a team made up of students, parents, teachers, support staff, and administrators. You need discretion and good judgment to be able to deal with their very different, and even conflicting, needs.

How to Break In

The first step toward a job as an administrative assistant in a school is to acquire the necessary office-management skills. Start practicing word processing in high school until you are accurate and fast. Learn a variety of software programs, such as PowerPoint (also of the Microsoft Office Suite).

Next, think about what kind of school you want to work in. Does a busy elementary school appeal to you? Would you enjoy dealing with young children, their parents, and teachers? Or would a middle school or high school atmosphere reflect your interests? What about a college or junior college office? Contact schools or districts directly. Parents, teachers, principals, and other administrative personnel are all useful contacts.

A Typical Day at Work

The office is the school nerve center, and more so in the mornings. Phones are ringing. Parents have questions about sports events and upcoming assessment tests. It's the start of a new semester and kids are walking in and out with schedule questions and mix-ups. Teachers are checking for mail and running worksheets off. The principal needs a grant request for after-school funds copied and postmarked today to meet the application deadline. There are attendance records to mark, and the attendance officer is out today. You have recruited an older student to help, with the enticement of community service hours, but you have to keep fielding questions from her. The start and end of the day are usually the busiest, and today is no exception.

You plan a teacher luncheon, fill out forms so the investments club can take their trip to a stock brokerage, and help yearbook students with some photo cropping. The morning passes quickly. Just before lunch, Jacob R. is sent to the office again. You have begun to recognize what to expect from him, based on how sullen he is. You make a point to chat with him after calling the principal to say she has a visitor. After all, he is always nice enough to you. The day is typical, in that you are needed.

Two-Year Training

Many community colleges offer two-year degrees in office administration or administrative services that prepare graduates to work in public schools as well as in private or community-run colleges. These programs are also offered by business schools and vocational-technical institutes. The best programs help you navigate the newest technologies, which help run offices optimally. Hopefully, you can add desktop publishing and Web design to your skills. Coursework should include training in the use of business mathematics and principles of accounting. A good program will also offer training in office procedures and information management. You will learn word processing at several levels and will be trained to run spreadsheets. Remember, you will be dealing with many people, so oral and written communication skills are important. In today's diverse school environment, knowing a foreign language will help make you invaluable.

What to Look For in a School

When considering a two-year school, be sure to ask these questions like these:

☞ Does the school offer a two-year program in office administration or administrative services?

☞ Are classes in keyboarding, online applications, and communications part of the program?

☞ Does the program include training in recent software applications?

☞ Are there opportunities to learn desktop publishing and Web design?

☞ Have any of the instructors worked recently in a school office?

☞ What is the record of the school's placement office?

The Future

An increase in office automation has made it possible to get more work done in fewer hours, so fewer office workers are needed in general. But schools will always need to replace retiring administrative assistants. Plus the nation is experiencing a trend toward the creation of new public, private, and charter schools. Future office opportunities will be best for qualified associate-level graduates who have knowledge of recent software applications, such as desktop publishing. Traditional skills will give way to more technical work, such as helping to maintain part of a school Web site. Despite these changes, doing a good job as an administrative assistant in a school still depends on good old-fashioned interpersonal skills, which are not easily automated. Administrative assistants will always play an important role, and schools will continue to look for responsible applicants who have a talent for juggling the many duties.

Job Seeking Tips

You can turn to Appendix A for general help with résumés and interviewing. Here are specific tips for becoming an administrative assistant.

✔ Meet early and often with the people in the career placement office at your school.

✔ Decide where you would most like to work—a preschool, an elementary school, a secondary school, or a college.

✔ Put together a résumé listing your office skills and proficiency in software applications.

✔ Volunteer in school offices in high school and college.

Interview with a Professional:
Q&A
Annie Perlmutter
School secretary, Oceanside, New York

Q: *How did you get started?*

A: I wanted to find a career with the same hours and locations as my husband, who's a gym teacher. I was in private industry, and I figured I could do the same in the schools, so, after I had my son Eric, I went to college, got my credits, and became a school secretary.

Q: *What's a typical day like?*

A: Well, it can be anything from absolute boredom to absolute chaos. I prefer a little chaos. I come in early, since I do all the paperwork—hiring teachers, scheduling, etc. Once the day begins, the phone is ringing, I have parents at the desk, wanting to see the principal, wanting to take their kids out of school—constantly all day long. Right now, I'm the only secretary in the office, so it's more towards the chaos side.

Q: *What's your advice for those starting this career?*

A: In this day and age, unless it's something you want to do for personal reasons like to be close to a spouse or for medical coverage, you're not going to make what you're going to make in private industry. The benefits are phenomenal, at least now, but there's not a lot of money—and they may extend the day, take away some of the benefits, etc.

Q: *What's the best part of the job?*

A: The vacations off and the hours!

Did You Know?

Of the clerical professionals who belong to the National Education Association, 25 percent work with special-education students.

Career Connections

For further information, contact the following organizations.

International Association of Administrative Professionals
http://www.iaap-hq.org

National Association of Educational Office Professionals
http://www.naeop.org

The NEA Foundation http://www.nfie.org

National Policy Board of Educational Administration http://www
.npbea.org

American Management Association http://www.amanet.org

Associate's Degree Programs

Search online for schools offering programs for becoming an administrative assistant. To get you started, here are a few:

Gibbs College, Boston, Massachusetts

Heald College, Honolulu, Hawaii

Missouri College, St. Louis, Missouri

Sullivan University, Lexington, Kentucky

Financial Aid

For more information on financing your education, turn to Appendix B. Be sure to contact your state board of education for scholarship, loan, and tuition exemption opportunities.

Related Careers

Administrative services manager, human resources assistant, library and media center assistant, office assistant, office manager, teacher, teacher aide, and tutor.

Vocational Education Instructor

Vital Statistics

Salary: The median annual salary for vocational education instructors is $45,570 a year, with the higher earners working in educational institutions, according to 2006 data from the U.S. Bureau of Labor Statistics.

Employment: Employment of vocational education instructors is expected to grow faster than the average for all occupations through 2014, according to the Bureau of Labor Statistics.

Education: Most schools require vocational certification or at least an associate's degree in vocational education, along with work experience in the field being taught. Expect to enroll in continuing education to stay current.

Work Environment: Classes are taught in vocational and technical departments, labs, and classrooms of high schools, community colleges, and other postsecondary schools. Some businesses, such as those that create computer hardware, hire teachers for on-the-job training.

Maybe your interest in cars is a defining part of who you are. Perhaps you are obsessed with cooking. Or maybe you like the idea of designing buildings but love working with people even more. What if you could combine your practical interests with a teaching career and help others realize their potential in the field that interests you most? You can as a vocational education teacher.

"The opportunities are excellent," says Chet Wichowski, of the Temple University Center for Career and Technical Education. "You can teach in private and public schools, adult education, or community college as well as internal trainers for business and industry or serving as test administrators."

Voc-ed instructors help adults and young adults develop the skills they need to get started in much-needed occupations, hundreds upon hundreds of posts in wide-ranging fields, such as automotive repair, business and computer skills, food service, medical technology, and merchandising. Secondary and postsecondary vocational teachers use their knowledge and experience in specific fields to prepare others to go out into the world with skills needed for steady employment.

Most states have guides that look at occupational requirements for voc-ed teachers, and these can vary. But "the typical vocational teacher comes in with several years of work experience, in addition to school experience," says Wichowski. With an associate's degree and a few year's related work behind you, your job prospects are better than most. You can become a much-needed voc-ed teacher and make a difference in many, many lives.

Maybe you don't see yourself as a traditional teacher, writing homework assignments on the blackboard and leading discussions on points of history or the meaning of a story. Fine: Voc-ed classrooms are designed to come alive with a steady flow of demonstrations and participatory exercises that prove and expand the students' skills. You show and tell, so your interest in the subject matter becomes a spark you pass along.

Maybe you have seen how tough teaching can be, just by attending a U.S. secondary school. But think about this: Compared with government and English classes, and all the other courses which are the regular requirements of a high school education, voc-ed classes by design attract only a population that is interested in the subject matter. Most students are there by choice.

In postsecondary vocational education classes, many students are enrolled because they are switching careers after learning more about the workforce; many others are new to the country and are eager to learn a new skill for a new place. Your expertise and authority are appreciated, not rallied against.

In 2004 there were 127,000 voc-ed jobs in postsecondary education alone, according to the Bureau of Labor Statistics, and many opportunities also exist in grade, middle, and high schools. Secondary and postsecondary schools are the major employers of voc-ed instructors, but factories, trade schools, business offices, and apprentice programs also hire vocational instructors. Trade organizations, such as those for hair stylists, often sponsor classes taught by vocational instructors for their members. Business organizations hire experts to keep their employees trained in recent technology.

On the Job

The job of a vocational education instructor is to plan and teach studies readying students for real employment. You determine which equipment, manuals, and tools are best for carrying out an effective program, and you follow through. Equipment should be in current use, the same kind the student is likely to find on the job. Printed material should reflect current methods and regulations.

Each voc-ed discipline has professional organizations that organize conferences and make research tools available. Teachers of broadcast production, for instance, will meet occasionally to see the latest tape machines being demonstrated. Likewise, in vocational education, instructors train students in the use of the "tools of the trade" by first demonstrating their use. For example, an instructor of welding uses a torch to piece together parts of a can. He or she carefully complies with rules of good safety and explains them step-by-step. A health instructor demonstrates the use of a stethoscope—and shows how you can warm the metal in your hand before applying it to someone's back.

Students are then given the opportunity to use these tools and equipment themselves. You note good and poor application. Using supportive language, you critique the students. Open and positive discussion of mistakes and a review of successes are equally important. You must take into account your students' level of familiarity with the subject matter. Beginners differ from those who are more interested in fine-tuning an advanced skill, and your classroom technique will change with each.

Newcomers need to know about the field, how it developed, and recent trends. They also need to know the professional standards they are expected to meet—and the requirements of states where they might work. Some jobs have specific privacy and ethical issues, such as those in health, which must be spelled out.

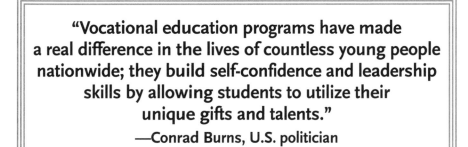

"Vocational education programs have made a real difference in the lives of countless young people nationwide; they build self-confidence and leadership skills by allowing students to utilize their unique gifts and talents."
—Conrad Burns, U.S. politician

Keys to Success

To be a successful vocational education instructor you should have

- experience in and a knowledge of a particular skill
- a talent for sharing what you know
- organizational skills
- excellent communication skills
- flexibility
- ideas for providing hands-on instruction

Do You Have What It Takes?

Practical experience in your skill—say it's electronics—is the main requirement. But also having degree or certification is preferred and often required. The job is best done by someone with a talent for motivating others. Older students often bring experience in other vocational fields to the classroom. A good instructor will appreciate and respect their contributions. The most important quality to have is an interest in passing on what you know and a desire to see your students succeed. Since you may be working with adults from a variety of backgrounds, it is important to have a talent for communication. A second language is a plus.

A Typical Day at Work

Your classroom is not typical, and your days aren't either. You probably won't place the desks in a row. You will be teaching in a space created to accommodate vocational teaching. It is likely to be a workshop filled with the tools of a trade. Let's say you teach the job skills of a dental technician. Your classroom resembles a dental office. It's Tuesday, and your class starts at 6 p.m., but you arrive two hours early to meet with someone who is repairing an X-ray machine. You have dovetailed that appointment with a meeting with a student who is seeking your advice about employment in a city in which you worked. You have already contacted a dentist you know and are able to offer an internship. As the class arrives, you greet the individuals and collect homework from those who missed the last session. These are adults with complicated adult lives, and their imperfect attendance is something you must work around.

How to Break In

First determine your area of expertise. Do you have experience in a skill that would make you attractive as a vocational education instructor? Or can you get it? As you train for a specific career area, volunteer to assist in a classroom with students below your level, say, in graphic design. Take whatever education courses you can take as long as they apply to secondary education. Be sure your program includes classes that teach solid education techniques. When your schooling is complete, keep yourself up-to-date with these practices:

✔ enrolling in continuing education classes

✔ attending conferences, graduate classes, and seminars in training development

✔ contacting local businesses who might be interested in training their employees in your field

Two-Year Training

Many community colleges offer one-year certificates or two-year associate's degree programs in vocational education. A program should include practical skills for career opportunities in a wide variety of subjects, such as air-conditioning repair, automotive repair, computers, data processing, electronics, food service, and medical technology. Often a period of supervised work is part of the program. On-the-job training offers students a chance to apply the skills learned in class. A good program also should offer classes that integrate the academic and vocational curriculum, such as math and science classes for students training in electronics or science and biology for those preparing for positions in health care. Classes in educational methods help vocational instructors handle the task of organizing a classroom and formally reviewing student progress. Cardiopulmonary resuscitation (CPR) and first aid will be part of a good curriculum.

What to Look For in a School

When considering a two-year school, be sure to ask these types of questions:

☞ Does the school offer certification or an associate's degree?

☞ Does the program include on-the-job training?

☞ Have the instructors worked in the field recently?

☞ Does the program offer classes in general education?

☞ What is the record of the school's placement office?

☞ Are the instructors available for career help?

☞ Is the equipment up-to-date and does it reflect current standards?

The Future

Since most adult and vocational education is funded by state or federal government, employment growth is affected by government budgets. Congress renewed the Carl D. Perkins Vocational and Technical Improvement Act in 2006, to last through 2012. Tech prep needs a separate funding stream, but the act authorized $1.3 billion for technical programs in 2006 alone. If you continue your education while you work, you can advance to an administrative position and continue teaching, in order to make more money and gain prestige. Voc-ed progress waned in the last two decades, so now the need to train young adults for entry-level jobs in practical fields has become critical, say government work-study sources. Demand is greater in community and junior colleges, but businesses increasingly provide work-related training for their employees to keep up with changing technology.

Did You Know?

Four out of every ten adults have participated in adult or vocational education in the past ten years.

—National Center for Education Statistics

Interview with a Professional:
Q&A
Jeff Wasson
Vocational education instructor (visual arts),
New York, New York

Q: *How did you get started?*

A: I got started because this is where I went to school. The staff there really liked my work ethic and there was a vacancy, so I was hired. In the beginning I was just doing the basic tasks, but as time went on it became apparent that I had a knack for teaching. I could communicate well with the students; I understood the material that needed to be taught really well and I was patient.

Q: *What's a typical day like?*

A: I walk around the studio and make sure everything is OK. If a student has a question or needs help, I assist them. Sometimes things are really busy, and I'm juggling multiple students, tasks, or problems.

Q: *What's your advice for those starting a career?*

A: Love what you do and know it inside and out. If you're in a competitive field, strive to be the best.

Q: *What's the best part of the job?*

A: When I show a student a technique and they run with it and do something I never would have thought of. Also, being able to make a living by teaching others how to make things, and being able to do that myself.

Job Seeking Tips

Follow these specific tips for vocational education, and then turn to Appendix A for help on résumés and interviewing:

✔ Determine what skill you are interested in and seek to maximize your experience.

✔ Talk to personnel departments at schools and community colleges about teaching opportunities and requirements.

✔ Contact trade and other organizations for your particular skill in order to network.

✔ Arrange volunteer teaching opportunities for yourself.

✔ Meet with the career placement officers at your school.

Career Connections

For further information, contact the following organizations.

Association for Career and Technical Education http://www .acteonline.org

ERIC Clearinghouse on Adult Career and Vocational Education http://www.ericacve.org

National Center for Research in Vocational Education http:// vocserve.berkeley.edu/OtherSites.html

Teachnology http://www.teach-nology.com/teachers/vocational_ed

U.S. Department of Education Office of Vocational and Adult Education http://www.ed.gov/about/offices/list/ovae/index.html?src=mr

Associate's Degree Programs

Search the Web for schools offering vocational education programs. Here are some ideas to get you started:

Art Institute of Las Vegas, Henderson, Nevada

Athens Technical College, Athens, Georgia

Pennsylvania College of Technology, Williamsport, Pennsylvania

Delaware Technical Community College, Dover, Delaware

Financial Aid

For general information about financial aid, turn to Appendix B, and many trustworthy sources can be found on the Internet. A sampling of scholarships is listed below.

Bristol Bay Native Corporation Education Foundation http://www.bbnc.net/education

Hawaii Community Foundation http://www.hawaiicommunity foundation.org

Kansas Regents http://kansasregents.org/financial_aid/awards.html

University of California 4-H Youth Development http://www.ca4h.org

Related Careers

Career counselor, computer technician, education administrators, manufacturing technician, office assistant, teacher aide, teacher, and tutor.

Library
Assistant

Vital Statistics

Salary: A library assistant earns a median hourly wage of about $10, or about $21,000 a year, according to 2006 data from the U.S. Bureau of Labor Statistics.

Employment: Job growth is predicted to be equal to the average for all occupations through 2014, according to the Bureau of Labor Statistics. But computer skills can help job seekers make the most of upcoming opportunities. Assistants with computer-related technical skills are in particular demand.

Education: An associate's degree will get your foot in the library door. Community colleges offer educational packages that mix library studies with liberal arts.

Work Environment: The setting varies. Work can occur in a quiet municipal library, a business setting, or a scholarly university library. School libraries are usually colorfully decorated and filled with kids.

In the village of Rye Brook, New York, officials recently commissioned a study for a new library. They were starting from scratch, with no building in mind and few preconceived notions. In newspaper editorials and e-mail exchanges, people wondered aloud: Should there be fewer books than usual? After all, so much literature is available online. So what does a forward-thinking library look like? A space pod with multiple screens and keyboards?

What do you think? Can you imagine ways that libraries might be evolving? A modern library aide must be comfortable recording data and conducting research on computers. This is just the latest in a long history of adaptations. Libraries started as collections of scrolls and art in ancient Mesopotamia and Egypt. They entertained few patrons. During the Middle Ages, library workers were monks, the few society members who could write. After Johannes Gutenberg invented the printing press in 1436, access to words and writing widened. These days, being a librarian is all about "information science."

A modern library is essentially a place to find information, but it also provides social glue. In a community library, people find leisure reading, track facts, use computers, and connect with words. School libraries are learning and social centers. Businesses, such as law and biotech firms, keep specialized libraries to streamline research.

Librarians generally have a master's in library science, but they make up just a third of library employees. The other two-thirds are workers with a variety of occupational responsibilities. Many are library assistants or technical assistants, jobs you can access with an associate's degree. Assistants now carry out many tasks that librarians have passed along. For the foreseeable future, work prospects for assistants are very good.

"The career paths for library assistants are better than average in that libraries are looking to retain a workforce that can assist them in helping to fulfill their missions as lifelong learning institutions," says Lorelle R. Swader, director for an American Library Association department called Human Resource Development and Recruitment.

An entry-level assistant may help patrons locate books, check volumes in and out, organize outreach programs, read aloud to children, or help older patrons search the Internet. With experience, an assistant assumes additional duties, such as specialized research and the supervision of other assistants. He or she may even manage a section of the library. Library assistants, clerical assistants, media assistants, aides, circulation assistants: These are a few of the titles for workers who organize library resources and help visitors. A job in a municipal or school library is great if you enjoy working with people, thrive on organization, and appreciate books and learning. You might also like working at a specialized site, such as an art or a biology library, in the educational or public sectors. And you're likely to find yourself thriving as well, because libraries tend to "grow" employees.

"I think library assistants [are] poised to be in a position to experience new possibilities for their own work and career development," says Swader.

On the Job

Many days are variations on the theme of organization: time at the circulation desk checking out books, periodicals, videotapes, and other material; accepting returned items; collecting fines for late fees; and issuing library cards to first-time visitors. You might also find yourself answering questions or referring patrons to someone on staff with specialized knowledge. As the day progresses, you shelve books and other material, keeping chaos at bay. You locate specifically requested material, perhaps from a branch library, and let patrons know when you have been successful. Your job becomes less clerical as you gain experience. Eventually a day might involve your instructing senior citizens on the use of the Internet. Or you might dive into research, such as tracing the history of local dog-walking laws for a group of pet owners who want to allow their animals off leash during certain hours. You might research book and film acquisitions or aid patrons with special needs, such as the visually challenged.

Very small libraries are sometimes operated by library assistants, so you might someday find yourself in charge of the entire show. Or you might operate a bookmobile, a van that takes media collections to senior citizen centers, remote neighborhoods, and other spots that lack their own libraries. In all cases, and from day one on the job, you will share your love of stories and information with a wide range of people. With the right attitude, the work can be as varied as all the people and all the information you come across in a lifetime—in other words, very much so!

> ## "He is wise who knows the sources of knowledge— where it is written and where it is to be found."
> —Archibald Alexander Hodge, Princeton professor

Keys to Success

To be a successful library assistant you should have
- a talent for dealing with people of all ages
- energy and enthusiasm
- computer and Internet research skills
- organizational ability
- an interest in books, magazines, and other media

Do You Have What It Takes?

Are you a people person, comfortable with both the young and the old? Do you have solid computer skills? Are you a big fan of books, magazines, and media of all sorts? Is information retrieval, or fact tracking, fun for you? Does looking things up feel like a game you can win? If you answered yes to these questions, consider the job of library assistant. It could be a terrific match for you.

Most public libraries are open weekends and some evenings, the times when working people can visit the stacks, so you may find you need to be flexible in your schedule. But your love of books, knowledge of reading and research, and interest in helping people are all going to help make this job feel like play.

How to Break In

Get at least a two-year degree in library science and liberal arts, to get the background needed to make intuitive jumps in a wide range of research. Be sure to take data information classes and sharpen computer skills. Take related part-time jobs, such as being a library page or bookstore seller. Think creatively along those lines. A library's public relations department might use volunteers as might its literacy program. If working in a school library interests you, try the volunteer route there too. Use these early experiences to familiarize yourself, as much as possible, with literature and the wider world.

Jobs may be found by applying directly to states, counties, cities, or school districts. Research the facilities that interest you. Contact the librarian at your community library or local school and strike up a conversation about the job, the needs of the library and others in the area, and the role that assistants play.

A Typical Day at Work

Adults come into the library to find books, high school students to research homework assignments, and young children to hear stories read aloud. Many patrons book time on the computer. On a typical day, you may find yourself at the main desk facing a line of visitors checking out or returning books. You might then switch assignments with another assistant and help visitors locate books, videos, or magazines. Some of your patrons will be in a rush to find what they need; that's the nature of modern life. You have to be patient and organized to address their needs efficiently. During quiet periods, you can take a breather. You might grab a coffee and sit and gab for a few minutes with your boss, just to refresh yourself.

In a school library, classes of children often arrive together, with or without their teacher and usually with a limited amount of time to accomplish their goals. It's likely that many need help finding materials and even staying on task. Some students might need your assistance coming up with ideas for research projects and plans for follow-through, so you have to be a teacher too. Toward day's end, you might help another assistant come up with a game plan for the library's volunteer staff. But no day goes exactly by the book in a busy library.

Two-Year Training

Community colleges offer certificates or associate's degree programs in library assistance. The name of the program will vary—from "library media technology" to "library science." But a good program provides a general background in humanities and the sciences. You should be offered technical and practical skills training for career opportunities in libraries of all kinds, including schools. You should be able to take courses in computer science, Microsoft Office Suite programs, and media equipment maintenance, cataloging and reference services, collection development, and more. You can concentrate on something, such as management or book-keeping, within the field. There are many ways to go. You might specialize in young adult and children's fiction—or in church librarianship. University libraries require more stringent course work, such as proficiency in a foreign language or advanced reference skills.

What to Look For in a School

When considering any two-year school, be sure to ask questions like these:

☞ Does the program provide a practical component such as an internship?

☞ Does the school offer courses in reference resources? Classification and cataloging?

☞ Have the instructors worked as librarians or library assistants recently?

☞ Does the program provide computer classes, such as in Microsoft Office Suite programs and Internet research?

☞ What is the record of the school's career-placement office?

The Future

Librarians are expected to have the business skills needed to run large facilities. As their oversight duties become more varied and complicated, there is similar movement among the assistants. Increasingly, assistants take on more targeted technical roles. The special skills you hone in school can help you enter a particular area of library operation and create a long-term career. You might be a whiz at public relations. It can serve you and your library well. Or you might be a technical genius. If so, you are needed to keep the computers operational and the Web site up to date.

Most library assistants are employed by local governments in public libraries or by schools, colleges, and universities. Since these libraries are less likely to be affected by the ups and downs of the business cycle, employment opportunities remain steady. Any assistant interested in advancement should show a willingness to assume added responsibilities.

Did You Know?

Mao Zedong (1893–1976) was a library assistant in Beijing. He ended up as chairman of the Chinese Communist Party. In the United States, J. Edgar Hoover's (1895–1972) first job was as a cataloger at the Library of Congress. He became head of the FBI.

Interview with a Professional:
Q&A
Sharyn Mondschein
Library assistant, Brooklyn, New York

Q: *How did you get started?*

A: I always liked to read. When I was in school, I got a job working in the library. I enjoyed it so much that I stayed with it, and it developed from there.

Q: *What's a typical day like?*

A: It's filled with many different kinds of tasks. In the morning I might find myself returning books to the shelves. I also enjoy helping people find the books that they need and want. Also I spend time at the desk checking out books. In a library there's always clerical work to do, and basically I just help out with anything that needs doing.

Q: *What's your advice for those starting this career?*

A: A library is a wonderful place to work. You need to be very well organized, and of course it goes without saying that you must have a love of people and books. Libraries are always looking for help from volunteers, and that's a good way to break in.

Q: *What's the best part of the job?*

A: The thing I love most is helping people find what they need. When I'm able to connect them with the books they're looking for, it makes me feel good.

Job Seeking Tips

Follow these specific tips for becoming a library assistant. You can turn to Appendix A for general help with résumés and interviewing.

✔ Meet with the counselors in the career placement office at your school.

✔ Join related professional groups.

✔ Share your interest with librarians at local public libraries and colleges.

✔ Contact state, county, city, and school district personnel departments.

✔ Be sure to emphasize in interviews and on your résumé what you have learned from related part-time work, such as a temporary job in a bookstore.

Career Connections

For information about jobs as a library assistant, contact your state library association directly. Also look up these organizations.

American Library Association http://www.ala.org/hrdr

Association for Library and Information Science Education http://www.alise.org/jobplacement/index.html

Council on Library/Media Technicians http://colt.ucr.edu/ltprograms.html

Special Libraries Association http://www.sla.org

Associate's Degree Programs

Search online for schools offering library assistant programs. To get you started, here are a few:

College of the Redwoods, Eureka, California

Ohio Dominican University, Columbus, Ohio

Rose State College, Midwest City, Oklahoma

North Hennepin Community College, Brooklyn Park, Minnesota

Financial Aid

Looking for scholarships? Here are a few that are or could be related to libraries. For more on financial aid for two-year programs, turn to Appendix B.

American Library Association http://www.ala.org/template.cfm?section=scholarships

California Library Association http://www.cla-net.org/awards/demco.php

Colorado Association of Libraries http://www.cal-webs.org/parascholarship.html

Nebraska Library Commission http://www.nlc.state.ne.us/nowhiring/scholarships.asp

Nevada Library Association http://nevadalibraries.org/organization/committees/scholarships.html

Related Careers

Health information technician, information and records clerk, librarian, medical records technician, office assistant, teacher aide, teacher, and tutor.

Social and Human Services Assistant

Vital Statistics

Salary: Median annual earnings for social and human service assistants range from $20,000 to $29,000, according to 2006 data from the U.S. Bureau of Labor Statistics.

Employment: Job opportunities in the social services industry, helping people with practical and special needs, are expected to be excellent. Work is available in agencies of all kinds. You will find many jobs available in state and local government too.

Education: An associate's degree, at minimum, will gain you access to related jobs. Work smart and earn further education to advance.

Work Environment: Social and human service assistants work in offices, clinics, hospitals, and group homes under the supervision of human service professionals.

Social and human service agencies improve the quality of life for people in need of a boost or some direction. Social and human services workers dedicate themselves to helping others. You might visit a homeless shelter to help link the families and individuals staying there to available medical care. You might call to make arrangements for emergency fuel to be delivered to a hard-luck family in time for cold weather. Other field calls might bring you to the offices of other community agencies or clinics, hospitals, outpatient clinics, rehabilitation programs, or shelters. As an assistant, you help clients meet their physical and medical needs. Their practical concerns become your mission.

"The work you do will probably be informational, getting and providing information for agencies," says Maria Ortiz, an administrator for the social work program at New Mexico State University. "A lot of the outreach work that is needed is covering the needs of clients and the community, providing links to counseling and to services."

Assistants are part advocate, caregiver, case manager, planner, and teacher. They forge relationships with and among families, groups, individuals, and communities. The original model for social work came to the United States from England during the Industrial Revolution and was formalized during the 19th century. In the beginning, this line of endeavor was called charity work. The 1950s and 1960s brought new ideas about helping the poor, the unemployed, and children or elderly people in need. The number of colleges and universities offering related degrees grew.

The tasks social and human services assistants perform are as varied as the clients they serve. Assistants determine eligibility for food stamps, Medicaid, or welfare (now called "Family Allowance"); schedule free meals; inspect foster-care homes; arrange transportation to medical treatment; update records; and interview clients. They provide emotional support and help clients further their own well-being and independence.

Entering the field with an associate's degree has its limits but can be a terrific first step. You can gain access to the work and see from inside where it is you want to go. You "can't always be licensed, but you can get community work," says Ortiz. Many agencies will readily hire someone with an associate's degree for some tasks instead of taking another person with a social work master's degree. It helps with their bottom line.

You may find the work emotionally draining. But if you are determined to make changes in the lives of people in need by helping them help themselves, you will be able to deal with related stresses. Social service employers depend on assistants who can communicate with a wide variety of clients, including the elderly, the ill, and people with disabilities. Clients can sometimes be difficult, especially if they have been frustrated in past attempts to get the help they need. It will be up to you to communicate with patience. You need to maintain a calm demeanor as you help them navigate the system. All that paperwork can be overwhelming, but that is why you are so needed.

On the Job

Assistants in the field of social and human services go by a variety of titles, including case management aide, community outreach worker, community support worker, human service worker, mental health aide, and social work assistant. They work under the direction of professionals in the fields of nursing, physical therapy, psychiatry, or social work. Some make on-site visits to client's homes, bringing food and medicine, checking on the conditions, and perhaps offering an open ear. Assistants in residential settings, halfway houses, or government-sponsored housing programs work in shifts and live part-time in these institutions.

In some jobs you work independently; others are closely supervised. The amount of responsibility you have is based on your education and experience, on laws pertaining to the field, and on the needs and expectations of your supervisors.

The job is busy and varied, no matter where you work. One moment you might visit a prospective foster parent. Another you begin the procedure for making sure a foster-care location is suitable, and on another you might pull files on a case of reported neglect. You might work in an agency, interviewing clients to determine how eligibility they are for public assistance and what their level of need is. There you would use knowledge of social service regulations to determine appropriate benefits, placements, or treatment plans. You consult with other professionals and other community agencies to obtain the most appropriate services for the people who have been assigned to you.

Assistants living and working in residential care or institutional settings lead groups, organize activities, and offer counseling and problem-solving services. You use your training to identify and assist clients in need of crisis intervention. Assistants working in the field visit the homes of clients to assist those who need help with daily living. They make sure medicines are taken correctly and on time; see that heat is available; and are company for those living alone.

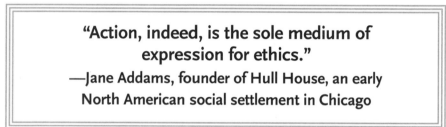

"Action, indeed, is the sole medium of expression for ethics."
—Jane Addams, founder of Hull House, an early North American social settlement in Chicago

Keys to Success

To be a successful social and human service assistant you should have
- a passion for helping others
- excellent written and oral communication skills
- patience and compassion
- a keen ability to prioritize
- strong organizational skills

Do You Have What It Takes?

Most human service administrators say what they look for in an assistant is a strong desire to help others and the ability to communicate well. These traits, plus a talent for using time effectively, are what you will need to do your best and be successful. There's a very good chance your caseload will be heavy. Record keeping and paperwork will be a major part of your work on the job. It will be important to keep yourself and your records organized. You must be able to make the best use of the time you have. Staff, clients, and their families are counting on you.

A Typical Day at Work

You will find that your day depends on what the moment brings—the needs or problems of scheduled and walk-in clients, the resources available in the community, and the emergency situations that arise. A morning spent in an agency or community center might find you determining a client's eligibility for food stamps. You typically can rely on your own knowledge of the social service system regulations and procedures to do this. However, this morning you find yourself facing a more complicated situation, one where you need to make some extra phone calls or consult with your supervisor or coworkers for additional guidance. As morning ends, you are in a meeting speaking up for a client who has been turned down for benefits due to an administrative mix-up. You have carefully recorded every step taken and the available information, in order to build your case. As lunch rolls around, you make plans to eat on the run with another services worker. The two of you have an afternoon field assignment, visiting a group home to check on the progress of a back-to-work program.

How to Break In

Do you want to work in an office where clients come to you with needs and you direct them toward help? Or can you see yourself as part of a residential treatment center team, working with clients who are struggling to get their lives together? Would you be comfortable working with older adults? Or would you prefer helping children with developmental disabilities? While you are in school, seek out volunteer work and classes in the areas most interesting to you. Not only will you gain experience, but you will begin to discover if the role is a good fit for you. The coursework and the training you receive with an associate's degree will make you familiar with the terms, the expectations, and the daily routine of the job. Once you have completed your training, stay in touch with teachers and fellow students. Keep up to date with state and county openings and regulations.

Two-Year Training

A two-year program in social work or human services will offer a core curriculum in human services, such as principles of sociology, general psychology, health and lifestyle, marriage and family relationships, and behavioral statistics. You will also cover courses in English, biology, and economics. A good program should also offer practical skills such as interviewing, recording information, conducting groups, utilizing community services, and advocating for clients. Supervised fieldwork or a practicum (much like an internship) at an agency or a variety of agencies is essential, so you know for certain the scope of the work before you long before you are responsible for the health and well-being of others. Students interested in specializing should be offered the opportunity to take courses in gerontology, child care, child protection, juvenile justice, corrections, and other such areas. Make sure the credits will transfer, should you decide to get additional training.

What to Look For in a School

When considering a two-year school, be sure to ask questions such as these:

☞ Does the school offer an associate degree in social work or human services?

☞ Does the program include supervised fieldwork?

☞ Are courses in specialized fields, such as gerontology or juvenile justice, offered?

☞ Have the instructors worked in the field of social services?

☞ Is it possible to transfer credits earned toward a four-year degree at the school or another school?

☞ What is the record of the school's placement office?

The Future

High demand for social and human services employees exists, especially for assistants. Employers increasingly rely on assistants to undertake responsibility for delivering services to clients. Employment opportunities should be particularly strong in private social-service agencies, which are frequently awarded contracts by public agencies to provide services such as adult day care and meal delivery. As the population ages, demand will also grow for assistants to work with the elderly. As additional mental and physical challenges are recognized, people who are "in the system" will increasingly require newly identified services. To advance to a position of more responsibility and better pay, further your education in counseling, human services, public policy, rehabilitation, or social work while you work. Some employers pay for courses and allow flexible scheduling for those pursuing them. Take advantage of all educational opportunities, including conferences.

Did You Know?

The first official social work class was offered in the summer of 1898 at Columbia University, in New York City.

Interview with a Professional:
Q&A

Panayiotis K. Venetis

Social and human services assistant,
Hawley, Pennsylvania

Q: *How did you get started?*

A: I actually got started by trying to figure out what I wanted to do with own my life. It was the dawn of my 20s. With a life of infinite possibilities before me, I found myself wanting to be many things, including a barbarian adventurer and a culture hero like Hercules. I had no idea how to translate these vague but powerful desires into some sort of a functional career. My work experiences were mainly in the food industry at the time. And avocationally I was extremely dedicated to obscure fringe topics and hands-on paranormal exploration.

Through the local Greek community I learned of an employment service that helped you sort these things out and then find a job that suited you. I made an appointment, was interviewed and assessed, oriented to their process, and then hired to work there. This was 27 years ago and I've always managed to keep one foot in this field.

It has taken me many years to actualize my own strange career goal. It is very satisfying to know that in the process I've helped countless others find and actualize theirs as well.

Q: *What's a typical day like?*

A: There really isn't a typical day. Right now I [work for] Northampton Community College's Workforce Literacy program in Wayne County, Pennsylvania. Folks are sent here to get assessed, become more marketable and work-ready, and to find direction toward a better future. I help them meet these challenges.

I'm also involved with NCC's Adult Literacy, Computer Literacy, and Family Literacy programs. Literacy plays a very large role in determining an individual's income level as well as the overall quality of life they can create for their family. We're extremely dedicated to helping people with improving their literacy and thereby gaining greater access to the opportunities that surround them.

I also [work with] other local literacy initiatives like the Wayne-Pike chapter of the First Book program, the Hawley Public Library, and our local YMCA.

The people I help are all individuals; their goals and timelines toward attainment are all quite different as well. The only common feature they share is that on some level they've decided to finally move forward or get unstuck. My challenge is to best use available resources and services to help them get there.

Q: *What's your advice for those starting this career?*

A: Dream *big*. Your imagination is your greatest ally, learn to use it to your advantage. Create bright pictures of what you want and let them pull you towards their attainment. Study the lives of people who have massively succeeded in the fields you wish to enter. Let these tales inspire and guide you on your journey. Don't worry about how long it will take; you'll get there, or somewhere better, if you don't give up. And learn to tune out the many nay-sayers in your life. This sounds like pie-in-the-sky positive thinking, but it actually works!

Q: *What's the best part of the job?*

A: The best part of the job is seeing others succeed, on their own terms. It is always gratifying to see a person who was lost find their way and actually win the bright prize they once glimpsed in their far future.

In my present position I *literally* celebrate their accomplishments publicly. How cool is that! And in helping others attain their goals, I learn many things that are helpful to me with attaining mine. Everybody wins, which is as it should be.

Job Seeking Tips

See the suggestions below and turn to Appendix A for advice on résumés and interviewing.

✔ Arrange internships, which can provide job leads.

✔ Meet regularly with the career placement officers at your school.

✔ Talk to people at all levels of private and public human services agencies about job opportunities.

✔ Contact state, county, and city departments of health and human services.

✔ Attend conferences sponsored by human service organizations to keep your skills up to date.

✔ Join or volunteer with a human services professional organization.

Career Connections

For further information contact the following organizations.

Clinical Social Work Association http://www.cswf.org

Council for Standards in Human Service Education http://www.cshse.org

National Association of Social Workers http://www.socialworkers.org

National Organization for Human Services
http://www.nationalhumanservices.org

School Social Work Association of America http://www.sswaa.org

Associate's Degree Programs

Search the Web for schools offering associate's degrees in human services or social work. To get started, look into these:

Barton Community College, Great Bend, Kansas

Casper College, Casper, Wyoming

Indiana University School of Social Work, Richmond, Indiana

Pennsylvania College of Technology, Williamsport, Pennsylvania

Financial Aid

Look in Appendix B for general information about financing your education. A short list (search the Web for more) of related scholarships and grants follows.

Blogging for Progress http://www.progressiveu.org

Indian Health Service, U.S. Department of Health and Human Services http://www.ihs.gov/JobsCareerDevelop/Jobs_index.asp

National Organization for Human Services http://www
.nationalhumanservices.org/scholarship.html

Related Careers

Child care worker, employment counselor, home health aide, nursing aide, occupational therapist aide, physical therapist aide, probation and parole officers, psychiatric aide, social worker, and teacher assistant.

Appendix A
Tools for Career Success

When 20-year-old Justin Schulman started job-hunting for a position as a fitness trainer—his first step toward managing a fitness facility—he didn't mess around. "I immediately opened the Yellow Pages and started calling every number listed under health and fitness, inquiring about available positions," he recalls. Schulman's energy and enterprise paid off: He wound up with interviews that led to several offers of part-time work.

Schulman's experience highlights an essential lesson for jobseekers: There are plenty of opportunities out there, but jobs won't come to you—especially the career-oriented, well-paying ones that that you'll want to stick with over time. You've got to seek them out.

Uncover Your Interests

Whether you're in high school or bringing home a full-time paycheck, the first step toward landing your ideal job is assessing your interests. You need to figure out what makes you tick. After all, there is a far greater chance that you'll enjoy and succeed in a career that taps into your passions, inclinations, and natural abilities. That's what happened with career-changer Scott Rolfe. He was already 26 when he realized he no longer wanted to work in the food industry. "I'm an avid outdoorsman," Rolfe says, "and I have an appreciation for natural resources that many people take for granted." Rolfe turned his passions into his ideal job as a forest technician.

If you have a general idea of what your interests are, you're far ahead of the game. You may know that you're cut out for a health care career, for instance, or one in business. You can use a specific volume of Top Careers in Two Years to discover what position to target. If you are unsure of your direction, check out the whole range of volumes to see the scope of jobs available. Ask yourself, what job or jobs would I most like to do if I *already* had the training and skills? Then remind yourself that this is what your two-year training will accomplish.

You can also use interest inventories and skills-assessment programs to further pinpoint your ideal career. Your school or public librarian or guidance counselor should be able to help you locate such assessments. Web sites such as America's Career InfoNet (http://www.acinet.org) and JobWeb (http://www.jobweb.com) also offer interest inventories. Don't forget the help advisers at any two-year college can provide to target your interests. You'll find suggestions for Web sites related to specific careers at the end of each chapter in any Top Careers in Two Years volume.

Unlock Your Network

The next stop toward landing the perfect job is networking. The word may make you cringe. But networking isn't about putting on a suit, walking into a roomful of strangers, and pressing your business card on everyone. Networking is simply introducing yourself and exchanging job-related and other information that may prove helpful to one or both of you. That's what Susan Tinker-Muller did. Quite a few years ago, she struck up a conversation with a fellow passenger on her commuter train. Little did she know that the natural interest she expressed in the woman's accounts payable department would lead to news about a job opening there. Tinker-Muller's networking landed her an entry-level position in accounts payable with MTV Networks. She is now the accounts payable administrator.

Tinker-Muller's experience illustrates why networking is so important. Fully 80 percent of openings are *never* advertised, and more than half of all employees land their jobs through networking, according to the U.S. Bureau of Labor Statistics. That's 8 out of 10 jobs that you'll miss if you don't get out there and talk with people. And don't think you can bypass face-to-face conversations by posting your résumé on job sites like Monster.com and Hotjobs.com and then waiting for employers to contact you. That's so mid-1990s! Back then, tens of thousands, if not millions, of job seekers diligently posted their résumés on scores of sites. Then they sat back and waited . . . and waited . . . and waited. You get the idea. Big job sites like Monster and Hotjobs have their place, of course, but relying solely on an Internet job search is about as effective as throwing your résumé into a black hole.

Begin your networking efforts by making a list of people to talk to: teachers, classmates (and their parents), anyone you've worked with, neighbors, worship acquaintances, and anyone you've interned or volunteered with. You can also expand your networking opportunities through the student sections of industry associations (listed at the end of each chapter of Top Careers in Two Years); attending or volunteering at industry events, association conferences, career fairs; and through job-shadowing. Keep in mind that only rarely will any of the people on your list be in a position to offer you a job. But whether they know it or not, they probably know someone who knows someone who is. That's why your networking goal is not to ask for a job but the name of someone to talk with. Even when you network with an employer, it's wise to say something like, "You may not have any positions available, but might you know someone I could talk with to find out more about what it's like to work in this field?"

Also, keep in mind that networking is a two-way street. For instance, you may be talking with someone who has a job opening that isn't appropriate for you. If you can refer someone else to the employer, either person may well be disposed to help you someday in the future.

Dial-Up Help

Call your contacts directly, rather than e-mail them. (E-mails are too easy for busy people to ignore, even if they don't mean to.) Explain that you're a recent graduate in your field; that Mr. Jones referred you; and that you're wondering if you could stop by for 10 or 15 minutes at your contact's convenience to find out a little more about how the industry works. If you leave this message as a voicemail, note that you'll call back in a few days to follow up. If you reach your contact directly, expect that they'll say they're too busy at the moment to see you. Ask, "Would you mind if I check back in a couple of weeks?" Then jot down a note in your date book or set up a reminder in your computer calendar and call back when it's time. (Repeat this above scenario as needed, until you get a meeting.)

Once you have arranged to talk with someone in person, prep yourself. Scour industry publications for insightful articles; having up-to-date knowledge about industry trends shows your networking contacts that you're dedicated and focused. Then pull together questions about specific employers and suggestions that will set you apart from the job-hunting pack in your field. The more specific your questions (for instance, about one type of certification versus another), the more likely your contact will see you as an "insider," worthy of passing along to a potential employer. At the end of any networking meeting, ask for the name of someone else who might be able to help you further target your search.

Get a Lift

When you meet with a contact in person (as well as when you run into someone fleetingly), you need an "elevator speech." This is a summary of up to two minutes that introduces who you are, as well as your experience and goals. An elevator speech should be short enough to be delivered during an elevator ride with a potential employer from the ground level to a high floor. In it, it's helpful to show that 1) you know the business involved; 2) you know the company; 3) you're qualified (give your work and educational information); and 4) you're goal-oriented, dependable, and hardworking. You'll be surprised how much information you can include in two minutes. Practice this speech in front of a mirror until you have the key points down very well. It should sound natural though, and you should come across as friendly, confident, and assertive. Remember, good eye contact needs to be part of your presentation as well as your everyday approach when meeting prospective employers or leads.

Get Your Résumé Ready

In addition to your elevator speech, another essential job-hunting tool is your résumé. Basically, a résumé is a little snapshot of you in words, reduced to one 8½ x 11-inch sheet of paper (or, at most, two sheets). You need a résumé whether you're in high school, college, or the workforce, and whether you've never held a job or have had many.

At the top of your résumé should be your heading. This is your name, address, phone numbers, and your e-mail address, which can be a sticking point. E-mail addresses such as sillygirl@yahoo.com or drinkingbuddy @hotmail.com won't score you any points. In fact they're a turn-off. So if you dreamed up your address after a night on the town, maybe it's time to upgrade. (Similarly, these days potential employers often check Myspace sites, personal blogs, and Web pages. What's posted there has been known to cost candidates a job offer.)

The first section of your résumé is a concise Job Objective (e.g., "Entry-level agribusiness sales representative seeking a position with a leading dairy cooperative"). These days, with word-processing software, it's easy and smart to adapt your job objective to the position for which you're applying. An alternative way to start a résumé, which some recruiters prefer, is to rework the Job Objective into a Professional Summary. A Professional Summary doesn't mention the position you're seeking, but instead focuses on your job strengths (e.g., "Entry-level agribusiness sales rep; strengths include background in feed, fertilizer, and related markets and ability to contribute as a member of a sales team"). Which is better? It's your call.

The body of a résumé typically starts with your Job Experience. This is a chronological list of the positions you've held (particularly the ones that will help you land the job you want). Remember: never, never any fudging. However, it is okay to include volunteer positions and internships on the chronological list, as long as they're noted for what they are.

Next comes your Education section. Note: It's acceptable to flip the order of your Education and Job Experience sections if you're still in high school or have gone straight to college and don't have significant work experience. Summarize the major courses in your degree area, any certifications you've achieved, relevant computer knowledge, special seminars, or other school-related experience that will distinguish you. Include your grade average if it's more than 3.0. Don't worry if you haven't finished your degree. Simply write that you're currently enrolled in your program (if you are).

In addition to these elements, other sections may include professional organizations you belong to and any work-related achievements, awards, or recognition you've received. Also, you can have a section for your interests, such as playing piano or soccer (and include any notable achievements regarding your interests, for instance, placed third in Midwest Regional Piano Competition). You should also note other special abilities, such as "Fluent in French" or "Designed own Web site." These sorts of activities will reflect well on you, whether or not they are job-related.

You can either include your references or simply note, "References upon Request." Be sure to ask your references permission to use their name and alert them to the fact that they may be contacted, before you include them on your résumé. For more information on résumé writing, check out Web sites such as http://www.resume.monster.com.

Craft Your Cover Letter

When you apply for a job either online or by mail, it's appropriate to include a cover letter. A cover letter lets you convey extra information about yourself that doesn't fit or isn't always appropriate in your résumé. For instance, in a cover letter, you can and should mention the name of anyone who referred you to the job. You can go into some detail about the reason you're a great match, given the job description. You also can address any questions that might be raised in the potential employer's mind (for instance, a gap in your résumé). Don't, however, ramble on. Your cover letter should stay focused on your goal: to offer a strong, positive impression of yourself and persuade the hiring manager that you're worth an interview. Your cover letter gives you a chance to stand out from the other applicants and sell yourself. In fact, 23 percent of hiring managers say a candidate's ability to relate his or her experience to the job at hand is a top hiring consideration, according to a Careerbuilder.com survey.

You can write a positive, yet concise cover letter in three paragraphs: An introduction containing the specifics of the job you're applying for; a summary of why you're a good fit for the position and what you can do for the company; and a closing with a request for an interview, contact information, and thanks. Remember to vary the structure and tone of your cover letter. For instance, don't begin every sentence with "I."

Ace Your Interview

Preparation is the key to acing any job interview. This starts with researching the company or organization you're interviewing with. Start with the firm, group, or agency's own Web site. Explore it thoroughly; read about their products and services, their history, and sales and marketing information.

Check out their news releases, links that they provide, and read up on or Google members of the management team to get an idea of what they may be looking for in their employees.

Sites such as http://www.hoovers.com enable you to research companies across many industries. Trade publications in any industry (such as *Food Industry News, Hotel Business,* and *Hospitality Technology*) are also available online or in hard copy at many college or public libraries. Don't forget to make a phone call to contacts you have in the organization to get an even better idea of the company culture.

Preparation goes beyond research, however. It includes practicing answers to common interview questions:

☞ *Tell me about yourself.* (Don't talk about your favorite bands or your personal history; give a brief summary of your background and interest in the particular job area.)

☞ *Why do you want to work here?* (Here's where your research into the company comes into play; talk about the firm's strengths and products or services.)

☞ *Why should we hire you?* (Now is your chance to sell yourself as a dependable, trustworthy, effective employee.)

☞ *Why did you leave your last job?* (This is not a talk show. Keep your answer short; never bad-mouth a previous employer. You can always say something simply such as, "It wasn't a good fit, and I was ready for other opportunities.")

Rehearse your answers, but don't try to memorize them. Responses that are natural and spontaneous come across better. Trying to memorize exactly what you want to say is likely to both trip you up and make you sound robotic.

As for the actual interview, to break the ice, offer a few pleasant remarks about the day, a photo in the interviewer's office, or something else similar. Then, once the interview gets going, listen closely and answer the questions you're asked, versus making any other point that you want to convey. If you're unsure whether your answer was adequate, simply ask, "Did that answer the question?" Show respect, good energy, and enthusiasm, and be upbeat. Employers are looking for people who are enjoyable to be around, as well as good workers. Show that you have a positive attitude and can get along well with others by not bragging during the interview, overstating your experience, or giving the appearance of being too self-absorbed. Avoid one-word answers, but at the same time don't blather. If you're faced with a silence after giving your response, pause for a few seconds, and then ask, "Is there anything else you'd like me to add?" Never look at your watch or answer your cellphone during an interview.

Near the interview's end, the interviewer is likely to ask you if you have any questions. Make sure that you have a few prepared, for instance:

☞ *"Tell me about the production process."*

☞ *"What's your biggest short-term challenge?"*

☞ *"How have recent business trends affected the company?"*

☞ *"Is there anything else that I can provide you with to help you make your decision?"*

☞ *"When will you make your hiring decision?"*

During a first interview, never ask questions like, "What's the pay?" "What are the benefits?" or "How much vacation time will I get?"

Find the Right Look

Appropriate dressing and grooming is also essential to interviewing success. For business jobs and many other occupations, it's appropriate to come to an interview in a nice (not stuffy) suit. However, different fields have various dress codes. In the music business, for instance, "business casual" reigns for many jobs. This is a slightly modified look, where slacks and a jacket are just fine for a guy, and a nice skirt and blouse and jacket or sweater are acceptable for a woman. Dressing overly "cool" will usually backfire.

In general, watch all of the basics from the shoes on up (no sneakers or sandals, and no overly high heels or short skirts for women). Also avoid attention-getting necklines, girls. Keep jewelry and other "bling" to a minimum. Tattoos and body jewelry are becoming more acceptable, but if you can take out piercings (other than in your ear), you're better off. Similarly, unusual hairstyles or colors may bias an employer against you, rightly or wrongly. Make sure your hair is neat and acceptable (get a haircut?). Also go light on the makeup, self-tanning products, body scents, and other grooming agents. Don't wear a baseball cap or any other type of hat; and by all means, take off your sunglasses!

Beyond your physical appearance, you already know to be well bathed to minimize odor (leave your home early if you tend to sweat, so you can cool off in private), make good eye contact, smile, speak clearly using proper English, use good posture (don't slouch), offer a firm handshake, and arrive within five minutes of your interview. (If you're unsure of where you're going, "Mapquest" it and consider making a dry-run to the site so you won't be late.) First impressions can make or break your interview.

Remember Follow-Up

After your interview, send a thank you note. This thoughtful gesture will separate you from most of the other candidates. It demonstrates your ability to follow through, and it catches your prospective employer's attention one more time. In a 2005 Careerbuilder.com survey, nearly 15 percent of 650 hiring managers said they wouldn't hire someone who failed to send a thank you letter after the interview. Thirty-two percent say they would still consider the candidate, but would think less of him or her.

So do you hand write or e-mail the thank you letter? The fact is that format preferences vary. One in four hiring managers prefer to receive a thank you note in e-mail form only; 19 percent want the e-mail, followed up with a hard copy; 21 percent want a typed hard-copy only; and 23 percent prefer just a handwritten note. (Try to check with an assistant on the format your potential employer prefers.) Otherwise, sending an e-mail and a handwritten copy is a safe way to proceed.

Winning an Offer

There are no sweeter words to a job hunter than, "We'd like to hire you." So naturally, when you hear them, you may be tempted to jump at the offer. *Don't.* Once an employer wants you, he or she will usually give you some time to make your decision and get any questions you may have answered. Now is the time to get specific about salary and benefits, and negotiate some of these points. If you haven't already done so, check out salary ranges for your position and area of the country on sites such as Payscale.com, Salary.com, and Salaryexpert.com (basic info is free; specific requests are not). Also, find out what sorts of benefits similar jobs offer. Then don't be afraid to negotiate in a diplomatic way. Asking for better terms is reasonable and expected. You may worry that asking the employer to bump up his offer may jeopardize your job, but handled intelligently, negotiating for yourself in fact may be a way to impress your future employer—and get a better deal for yourself.

After you've done all the hard work that successful job-hunting requires, you may be tempted to put your initiative into autodrive. However, the efforts you made to land your job-from clear communication to enthusiasm—are necessary now to pave your way to continued success. As Danielle Little, a human-resources assistant, says, "You must be enthusiastic and take the initiative. There is an urgency to prove yourself and show that you are capable of performing any and all related tasks. If your manager notices that you have potential, you will be given additional responsibilities, which will help advance your career." So do your best work on the job, and build your credibility. Your payoff will be career advancement and increased earnings.

Appendix B

Financial Aid

One major advantage of earning a two-year degree is that it is much less expensive than paying for a four-year school. Two years is naturally going to cost less than four, and two-year graduates enter the workplace and start earning a paycheck sooner than their four-year counterparts.

The latest statistics from the College Board show that average yearly total tuition and fees at a public two-year college is $2,191, compared to $5,491 at a four-year public college. That cost leaps to more than $21,000 on average for a year at a private four-year school.

With college costs relatively low, some two-year students overlook the idea of applying for financial aid at all. But the fact is, college dollars are available whether you're going to a trade school, community college, or university. About a third of all Pell Grants go to two-year public school students, and while two-year students receive a much smaller percentage of other aid programs, the funding is there for many who apply.

How Does Aid Work?

Financial aid comes in two basic forms: merit-based and need-based.

Merit-based awards are typically funds that recognize a particular talent or quality you may have, and they are given by private organizations, colleges, and the government. Merit-based awards range from scholarships for good writing to prizes for those who have shown promise in engineering. There are thousands of scholarships available for students who shine in academics, music, art, science, and more. Resources on how to get these awards are provided later in this chapter.

Need-based awards are given according to your ability to pay for college. In general, students from families that have less income and fewer assets receive more financial aid. To decide how much of this aid you qualify for, schools look at your family's income, assets, and other information regarding your finances. You provide this information on a financial aid form—usually the federal government's Free Application for Federal Student Aid (FAFSA). Based on the financial details you provide, the school of your choice calculates your Expected Family Contribution (EFC). This is the amount you are expected to pay toward your education each year.

Once your EFC is determined, a school uses this simple formula to figure out your financial aid package:

Cost of attendance at the school
- **Your EFC**
- **Other outside aid (private scholarships)**
= **Need**

Schools put together aid packages that meet that need using loans, work-study, and grants.

Know Your School

When applying to a school, it's a good idea to find out their financial aid policy and history. Read over the school literature or contact the financial aid office and find out the following:

✔ *Is the school accredited?* Schools that are not accredited usually do not offer as much financial aid and are not eligible for federal programs.

✔ *What is the average financial aid package at the school?* The typical award size may influence your decision to apply or not.

✔ *What are all the types of assistance available?* Check if the school offers federal, state, private, or institutional aid.

✔ *What is the school's loan default rate?* The default rate is the percentage of students who took out federal student loans and failed to repay them on time. Schools that have a high default rate are often not allowed to offer certain federal aid programs.

✔ *What are the procedures and deadlines for submitting financial aid?* Policies can differ from school to school.

✔ *What is the school's definition of satisfactory academic progress?* To receive financial aid, you have to maintain your academic performance. A school may specify that you keep up at least a C+ or B average to keep getting funding.

✔ *What is the school's job placement rate?* The job placement rate is the percentage of students who find work in their field of study after graduating.

You'll want a school with a good placement rate so you can earn a good salary that may help you pay back any student loans you have.

Be In It to Win It

The key to getting the most financial aid possible is filling out the forms, and you have nothing to lose by applying. Most schools require that you file the FAFSA, which is *free* to submit, and you can even do it online. For more information on the FAFSA, visit the Web site at http://www.fafsa.ed.gov. If you have any trouble with the form, you can call 1-800-4-FED-AID for help.

To receive aid using the FAFSA, you must submit the form soon after January 1 prior to the start of your school year. A lot of financial aid is delivered on a first-come, first-served basis, so be sure to apply on time.

Filing for aid will require some work to gather your financial information. You'll need details regarding your assets and from your income tax forms, which include the value of all your bank accounts and investments. The form also asks if you have other siblings in college, the age of your parents, or if you have children. These factors can determine how much aid you receive.

Three to four weeks after you submit the FAFSA, you receive a document called the Student Aid Report (SAR). The SAR lists all the information you provided in the FAFSA and tells you how much you'll be expected to contribute toward school, or your Expected Family Contribution (EFC). It's important to review the information on the SAR carefully and make any corrections right away. If there are errors on this document, it can affect how much financial aid you'll receive.

The Financial Aid Package

Using information on your SAR, the school of your choice calculates your need (as described earlier) and puts together a financial aid package. Aid packages are often built with a combination of loans, grants, and work-study. You may also have won private scholarships that will help reduce your costs.

Keep in mind that aid awarded in the form of loans has to be paid back with interest just like a car loan. If you don't pay back according to agreed upon terms, you can go into *default*. Default usually occurs if you've missed payments for 180 days. Defaulted loans are often sent to collection agencies, which can charge costly fees and even take money owed out of your wages. Even worse, a defaulted loan is a strike on your credit history. If you have a negative credit history, lenders may deny you a mortgage, car loan, or other personal loan. There's also financial incentive for paying back on time— many lenders will give a 1 percent discount or more for students who make consecutive timely payments. The key is not to borrow more than you can afford. Know exactly how much your monthly payments will be on a loan when it comes due and estimate if those monthly payments will fit in your future budget. If you ever do run into trouble with loan payments, don't hesitate to contact your lender and see if you can come up with a new payment arrangement—lenders want to help you pay rather than see you go into default. If you have more than one loan, look into loan consolidation, which can lower overall monthly payments and sometimes lock in interest rates that are relatively low.

The Four Major Sources of Aid

U.S. Government Financial Aid

The federal government is the biggest source of financial aid. To find all about federal aid programs, visit http://www.studentaid.fed.gov or call 1-800-4-FED-AID with any questions. Download the free brochure *Funding Education Beyond High School,* which tells you all the details on federal programs. To get aid from federal programs you must be a regular student working toward a degree or certificate in an eligible program. You also have to have a high school diploma or equivalent, be a U.S. citizen or eligible noncitizen and have a valid Social Security number (check http://www.ssa.gov for info). If you are a male aged 18–25, you have to register for the Selective Service. (Find out more about that requirement at http://www.sss.gov or call 1-847-688-6888.) You must also certify that you are not in default on a student loan and that you will use your federal aid only for educational purposes.

Some specifics concerning federal aid programs can change a little each year, but the major programs are listed here and the fundamentals stay the same from year to year. (Note that amounts you receive generally depend on your enrollment status—whether it be full-time or part-time.)

Pell Grant
For students demonstrating significant need, this award has been ranging between $400 and $4,050. The size of a Pell grant does not depend on how much other aid you receive.

Supplemental Educational Opportunity Grant (SEOG)
Again for students with significant need, this award ranges from $100 to $4,000 a year. The size of the SEOG can be reduced according to how much other aid you receive.

Work-Study
The Federal Work-Study Program provides jobs for students showing financial need. The program encourages community service and work related to a student's course of study. You earn at least minimum wage and are paid at least once a month. Again, funds must be used for educational expenses.

Perkins Loans
With a low interest rate of 5 percent, this program lets students who can document the need borrow up to $4,000 a year.

Stafford Loans
These loans are available to all students regardless of need. However, students with need receive *subsidized* Staffords, which do not accrue interest while you're in school or in deferment. Students without need can take *unsubsidized* Staffords, which do accrue interest while you are in school or in deferment. Interest rates vary but can go no higher than 8.25 percent. Loan amounts vary too, according to what year of study you're in and whether you are financially dependent on your parents or not. Students defined as independent of their parents can borrow much more. (Students who have their own kids are also defined as independent. Check the exact qualifications for independent and dependent status on the federal government Web site http://www.studentaid.fed.gov.)

PLUS Loans
These loans for parents of dependent students are also available regardless of need. Parents with good credit can borrow up to the cost of attendance minus any other aid received. Interest rates are variable but can go no higher than 9 percent.

Tax Credits
Depending on your family income, qualified students can take federal tax deductions for education with maximums ranging from $1,500 to $2,000.

Americorps
This program provides full-time educational awards in return for community service work. You can work before, during, or after your postsecondary education and use the funds either to pay current educational expenses or to repay federal student loans. Americorps participants work assisting teachers in Head Start, helping on conservation projects, building houses for the homeless, and doing other good works. For more information, visit http://www.americorps.gov

State Financial Aid

All states offer financial aid, both merit-based and need-based. Most states use the FAFSA to determine eligibility, but you'll have to contact your state's higher education agency to find out the exact requirements. You can get contact information for your state at http://www.bcol02.ed.gov/Programs/EROD/org_list.cfm. Most of the state aid programs are available only if you study at a school in the state where you reside. Some states are very generous, especially if you're attending a state college or university. California's Cal Grant program gives needy state residents free tuition at in-state public universities.

School-Sponsored Financial Aid

The school you attend may offer its own loans, grants, and work programs. Many have academic- or talent-based scholarships for top-performing students. Some two-year programs offer cooperative education opportunities where you combine classroom study with off-campus work related to your major. The work gives you hands-on experience and some income, ranging from $2,500 to $15,000 per year depending on the program. Communicate with your school's financial aid department and make sure you're applying for the most aid you can possibly get.

Private Scholarships

While scholarships for students heading to four-year schools may be more plentiful, there are awards for the two-year students. Scholarships reward students for all sorts of talent—academic, artistic, athletic, technical, scientific, and more. You have to invest time hunting for the awards that you might qualify for. The Internet now offers many great scholarship search services. Some of the best ones are:

The College Board (http://www.collegeboard.com/pay)

FastWeb! (http://www.fastweb.monster.com)

MACH25 (http://www.collegenet.com)

Scholarship Research Network (http://www.srnexpress.com)

SallieMae's College Answer (http://www.collegeanswer.com)

Note: Be careful of scholarship-scam services that charge a fee for finding you awards but end up giving you nothing more than a few leads that you could have gotten for free with a little research on your own. Check out the Federal Trade Commission's Project ScholarScam (http://www.ftc.gov/bcp/conline/edcams/scholarship).

In your hunt for scholarship dollars, be sure to look into local community organizations (the Elks Club, Lions Club, PTA, etc.), local corporations, employers (your employer or your parents' may offer tuition assistance), trade groups, professional associations (National Electrical Contractors Association, etc.), clubs (Boy Scouts, Girl Scouts, Distributive Education Club of America, etc.), heritage organizations (Italian, Japanese,

Chinese, and other groups related to ethnic origin), church groups, and minority assistance programs.

Once you find awards you qualify for, you have to put in the time applying. This usually means filling out an application, writing a personal statement, and gathering recommendations.

General Scholarships

A few general scholarships for students earning two-year degrees are

Coca-Cola Scholars Foundation, Inc.

Coca-Cola offers 350 thousand-dollar scholarships (http://www.coca colascholars.org) per year specifically for students attending two-year institutions.

Phi Theta Kappa (PTK)

This organization is the International Honor Society of the Two-Year College. PTK is one of the sponsors of the All-USA Academic Team program, which annually recognizes 60 outstanding two-year college students (http://scholarships.ptk.org). First, Second, and Third Teams, each consisting of 20 members, are selected. The 20 First Team members receive stipends of $2,500 each. All 60 members of the All-USA Academic Team and their colleges receive extensive national recognition through coverage in *USA TODAY*. There are other great scholarships for two-year students listed on this Web site.

Hispanic Scholarship Fund (HSF)

HSF's High School Scholarship Program (http://www.hsf.net/scholar ship/programs/hs.php) is designed to assist high school students of Hispanic heritage obtain a college degree. It is available to graduating high school seniors who plan to enroll full-time at a community college during the upcoming academic year. Award amounts range from $1,000 to $2,500.

The Military

All branches of the military offer tuition dollars in exchange for military service. You have to decide if military service is for you. The Web site http://www.myfuture.com attempts to answer any questions you might have about military service.

Lower Your Costs

In addition to getting financial aid, you can reduce college expenses by being a money-smart student. Here are some tips.

Use Your Campus

Schools offer perks that some students never take advantage of. Use the gym. Take in a school-supported concert or movie night. Attend meetings and lectures with free refreshments.

Flash Your Student ID

Students often get discounts at movies, museums, restaurants, and stores. Always be sure to ask if there is a lower price for students and carry your student ID with you at all times. You can often save 10 to 20 percent on purchases.

Budget Your Funds

Writing a budget of your income and expenses can help you be a smart spender. Track what you buy on a budget chart. This awareness will save you dollars.

Share Rides

Commuting to school or traveling back to your hometown? Check and post on student bulletin boards for ride shares.

Buy Used Books

Used textbooks can cost half as much as new. Check your campus bookstore for deals and also try http://www.eCampus.com and http://www.bookcentral.com

Put Your Credit Card in the Freezer

That's what one student did to stop overspending. You can lock your card away any way you like, just try living without the ease of credit for awhile. You'll be surprised at the savings.

A Two-Year Student's Financial Aid Package

Minnesota State Colleges and Universities provides this example of how a two-year student pays for college. Note how financial aid reduces his out-of-pocket cost to about $7,000 per year.

Jeremy's Costs for One Year

Jeremy is a freshman at a two-year college in the Minnesota. He has a sister in college, and his parents own a home but have no other significant savings. His family's income: $42,000.

College Costs for One Year

Tuition	$3,437
Fees	$388
Estimated room and board*	$7,200
Estimated living expenses**	$6,116
Total cost of attendance	*$17,141*

Jeremy's Financial Aid

Federal grants (does not require repayment)	$2,800
Minnesota grant (does not require repayment)	$676
Work-study earnings	$4,000
Student loan (requires repayment)	$2,625
Total financial aid	*$10,101*

Total cost to Jeremy's family	*$7,040*

* Estimated cost reflecting apartment rent rate and food costs. The estimates are used to calculate the financial aid. If a student lives at home with his or her parents, the actual cost could be much less, although the financial aid amounts may remain the same.

** This is an estimate of expenses including transportation, books, clothing, and social activities.

Index

A

alcohol abuse counselor. *See* drug/alcohol abuse counselor
American Sign Language (ASL), 28
ASL. *See* American Sign Language
assistant
    checking with, 92
    entry-level, 70
    library, 68–75
    school administrative, 52–59
    social/human services, 76–84
    teacher, 10–17
associate's degree program
    child care worker, 50
    cost of, xv, 100–101
    drug/alcohol abuse counselor, 25–26
    edge gained with, xiv
    library assistant, 75
    limits of, 78
    preschool teacher, 8
    recreation worker, 42
    school administrative assistant, 59
    sign language interpreter, 34
    social/human services assistant, 84
    teacher assistant, 17
    vocational education instructor, 67

B

benefits, 92. *See also* insurance
    child care worker, 49
    determining, 79
    school administrative assistant, 58

bilingual
    employment, 47
    preschool teacher, 2
breaking in
    as child care worker, 47
    as drug/alcohol abuse counselor, 22
    as library assistant, 71–72
    as preschool teacher, 5
    as recreation worker, 38–39
    as school administrative assistant, 55–56
    as sign language interpreter, 30–31
    as social/human services assistant, 80
    as teacher assistant, 14
    as vocational education instructor, 64

C

cardiopulmonary resuscitation. *See* CPR
career. *See also* career connections; related careers
    direction, xii–xiii
    goals, 82
    paths, 70
    plan, xi
    selection, xvi
    success, 85–92
    Web sites, 86
career connections
    child care worker, 50
    drug/alcohol abuse counselor, 25
    library assistant, 75
    preschool teacher, 8

recreation worker, 41

school administrative assistant, 58–59

sign language interpreter, 33–34

social/human services assistant, 83

teacher assistant, 16–17

vocational education instructor, 67

case management aid. *See* social/human
 services assistant

certification, 25

child care worker, 43–51

 benefits, 49

 federally funded, 44

 financial aid, 50–51

 regulations, 48

 tasks of, 45–46

 training, 47–48

childhood

 development, 5

 education, 2, 45

 research, 3, 44

 statistics, 48

classes, xv

clerical work, 74

coaching, 37

college expenses, 99–100

communication

 e-mail, 87

 flow of, 54

 skills, xii

 supervisor, 46

community college. *See also* four-year
 degree program; two-year degree
 program

 internships, 39

 teacher, 61

community service, 97

 computers

 skills, 71

 teacher assistant help with, 13

counselor

 drug/alcohol abuse, 18–26

peer, 22

coursework, xii

cover letter, 89

CPR (cardiopulmonary resuscitation), 65

creativity, xii

D

day care

 childhood attendance of, 3

 organizations, 44

design, 56

dress, 91

drug/alcohol abuse counselor, 18–26

 certification, 25

 financial aid, 26

 license, 19

 prevention focus from, 21

 record keeping, 24

 supervisor, 23

 tasks of, 20–21

 training, 22

E

education

 awards, 97

 childhood, 2, 45

 nighttime, xv

 opportunities in, 81

 organization, 53–54

 special, 11

 statistics, 15

EFC. *See* expected family contribution

e-mail

 addresses, 88

 communication, 87

 thank you letter by, 92

employment. *See also* unemployment

 bilingual, 47

 luxury, 40

 self, 20

enrollment statistics, xiv

entry-level assistant, 70
equipment
   setting up, 12
   troubleshooting, 54
   up-to-date, 62
expected family contribution (EFC), 93,
   95

F
FAFSA (Free Application for Federal
   Student Aid), 93, 95
federal funding
   for child care worker, 44
   for vocational education instructor, 65
financial aid, 93–101. *See also* federal
   funding; scholarships
   child care worker, 50–51
   drug/alcohol abuse counselor, 26
   example of, 100–101
   library assistant, 75
   package, 95–96
   preschool teacher, 8
   recreation worker, 42
   research, 94
   school administrative assistant, 59
   school-sponsored, 98
   sign language interpreter, 34
   social/human services assistant, 84
   state, 97–98
   statistics, 101
   teacher assistant, 17
   U.S. government, 96–97
   vocational education instructor, 67
   Web sites, 95–100
follow-up, 91–92
foreign language. *See* bilingual
four-year degree program
   expense of, 93
   two-year degree program v., xv
future
   child care workers, 48

drug/alcohol abuse councilors, 23
   library assistants, 73
   planning, xvi
   preschool teachers, 6
   recreation workers, 40
   school administrative assistants, 57
   sign language interpreters, 32
   social/human services assistants, 81
   teacher assistants, 15
   vocational education instructors, 65

G
goals, 82
grounds maintenance, 37

H
handicaps, students with, 12

I
information science. *See* library assistant
instructor. *See* vocational education
   instructor
insurance, 49
Internet
   classes, xv
   reliance on, 86
   research, xi
internships, 39
interpreter. *See* sign language interpreter
interview
   acing, 89–91
   child care worker, 49
   drug/alcohol abuse counselor, 24–25
   library assistant, 74
   preparation, 87
   preschool teacher, 7
   recreation worker, 41
   research, 89–90
   school administrative assistant, 58
   sign language interpreter, 33
   social/human services assistant, 82–83

success, 91
teacher assistant, 16
vocational education instructor, 66

J
jobs
management, xiv
searching, xvi
job seeking tips
child care worker, 49–50
drug/alcohol abuse counselor, 23
eye contact, 88
library assistant, 74
preschool teacher, 7–8
recreation worker, 40
school administrative assistant, 57
sign language interpreter, 32
social/human services assistant, 83
teacher assistant, 16
vocational education instructor, 66

L
library assistant, 68–75
clerical work, 74
financial aid, 75
forward thinking, 69
research done by, 71
specialization, 73
tasks of, 70–71
training, 72

M
maintenance, 37
management jobs, xiv
medical care, 77
motivation, 38

N
networking, 87
No Child Left Behind Act, 14

O
organization(s)
day care, 44
education, 53–54
record, 79
recreation worker, 41
thrive on, 70
trade, 62

P
paraprofessional. *See* teacher assistant
part-time work, xi, 5, 31
peer counseling, 22
placement rate, 94
practical experience, 63
preschool teacher(s), 1–9
bilingual, 2
diversity celebrated by, 4
financial aid, 8
methods, 7
supervisor, 6
tasks of, 3–4
training, 5–6
privacy, 21
promotion, 81
public speaking, 31

Q
qualifications
child care worker, 46
drug/alcohol abuse counselor, 22
library assistant, 71
preschool teacher, 4
recreation worker, 38
school administrative assistant, 55
sign language interpreter, 30
social/human services assistant, 79
teacher assistant, 13
vocational education instructor,
63–64

R

recreation worker, 35–42
  financial aid, 42
  luxury liners, 40
  motivation supplied by, 38
  organization, 41
  supervisor, 36
  tasks of, 37–38
  training, 39–40
referrals, 24
registration, 53
regulations, 48
related careers
  child care worker, 51
  drug/alcohol abuse counselor, 26
  library assistant, 75
  preschool teacher, 9
  recreation worker, 42
  school administrative assistant, 59
  sign language interpreter, 34
  social/human services assistant, 84
  teacher assistant, 17
  vocational education instructor, 67
requirements, 61
research
  childhood, 3, 44
  financial aid, 94
  Internet, xi
  interview, 89–90
  library assistant doing, 71
resources, 83
résumé, 88
routine, 45

S

salary
  child care workers, 44
  drug/alcohol abuse councilors, 19
  library assistants, 69
  negotiation, 92
  preschool teachers, 2

public v. private industry, 58
range, xii
  recreation workers, 36
  school administrative assistants, 53
  sign language interpreters, 28
  social/human services assistants, 77
  statistics, xiii
  supervisor, 25
  teacher assistants, 11
  vocational education instructors, 61
schedule, 78
scholarships
  forms of, 93–94
  general, 99
  private, 98–99
school administrative assistant, 52–59
  automation replacing, 57
  benefits, 58
  financial aid, 59
  guidance provided by, 53
  multitasking as, 55
  tasks of, 54–55
  training, 56
self-employment, 20
shadowing, 29
sick days, 49
sign language interpreter(s), 27–34
  financial aid, 34
  injuries, 30
  invisibility of, 33
  shortage of, 32
  specialization, 28
  tasks of, 29–30
  training, 31
skills
  communication, xii
  computer, 71
  technical, xiii
social/human services assistant, 76–84
  crisis intervention by, 79
  financial aid, 84

literacy advocated by, 82
promotion, 81
quality of life improved by, 77
requirements, 61
resources, 83
tasks of, 78–79
training, 80–81
speaking publicly, 31
special education, 11
specialization
  library assistant, 73
  sign language interpreter, 28
statistics
  child care worker, 44
  childhood, 48
  drug/alcohol abuse counselor, 19
  education, 15
  enrollment, xiv
  hiring, 89
  labor, 86
  library assistant, 69
  preschool teacher, 2
  recreation worker, 36
  salary, xiii
  school administrative assistant, 53
  sign language interpreter, 28
  social/human services assistant, 77
  teacher assistant, 11
  tuition, 101
  vocational education instructor, 61
stress, 78
student
  handicapped, 12
  teacher, 7
substance abuse. *See* drug/alcohol abuse
  counselor
success
  career, 85–92
  child care worker, 46
  drug/alcohol abuse counselor, 20
  interview, 91

library assistant, 71
preschool teacher, 4
recreation worker, 38
school administrative assistant, 55
sign language interpreter, 30
social/human services assistant, 79
teacher assistant, 13
vocational education instructor, 63
supervisor
  communication, 46
  drug/alcohol abuse counselor, 23
  preschool teacher, 6
  recreation worker, 36
  salary of, 25

T
teacher
  community college, 61
  preschool, 1–9
  student, 7
  teacher assistant relied on by, 15
teacher assistant, 10–17
  computer help from, 13
  energy needed by, 16
  financial aid, 17
  tasks of, 12–13
  teacher reliance on, 15
  technology, 11
  training, 14–15
technical skills, xiii
technology
  teacher assistant, 11
  training, 62
tools, 85–92
Top Careers in Two Years, 85–86
trade organizations, 62
training
  child care worker, 47–48
  drug/alcohol abuse counselor, 22
  library assistant, 72
  paying for, xvi

preschool teacher, 5–6
recreation worker, 39–40
school administrative assistant, 56
sign language interpreter, 31
social/human services assistant, 80–81
teacher assistant, 14–15
technology, 62
vocational education instructor, 64–65
tuition statistics, 101
tutoring, xi
two-year degree program
    considerations, 6, 15, 23, 32, 40, 48,
        57, 65, 73, 81
    cost example, 100
    flexibility provided by, xv
    four-year degree program v., xv
    pro's of, 93
typical workday
    child care workers, 47
    drug/alcohol abuse councilors, 21
    library assistants, 72
    preschool teachers, 5
    recreation workers, 39
    school administrative assistants, 56
    sign language interpreters, 31
    social/human services assistants, 80
    teacher assistants, 14
    vocational education instructors, 64

U
unemployment, xiii

V
vacation, 49
vocational education instructor, 60–67
    competition faced by, 66
    federally funded, 65
    financial aid, 67
    practical experience prized by, 63
    requirements, 61
    tasks of, 62–63
    training, 64–65
volunteering, 5, 31, 72

W
Web sites, xiv, xv, 89–92
    career, 86
    designing, 56
    financial aid, 95–100
worker
    child care, 43–51
    part-time, xi, 5, 31
    recreation, 35–42
work-study, 96–97